Audition Scenes for Students

Edited with Notes

by

JOHN WRAY YOUNG

THE DRAMATIC PUBLISHING COMPANY

CHICAGO

FOR MOTHER AND DAD--

Since it was Dr. and Mrs. John Wray Young

who first showed me the wonder of theatre

Other Books by JOHN WRAY YOUNG

THE COMMUNITY THEATRE and HOW IT WORKS

DIRECTING THE PLAY from SELECTION
TO OPENING NIGHT

HOW TO PRODUCE THE PLAY
(with MARGARET MARY YOUNG)

CONTENTS

BEFORE THE CURTAIN

For One Actor

LOOK BACK IN ANGER......... John Osborne
serious
CYRANO DE BERGERAC..... Edmond Rostand
melodrama
LUTHER.......................John Osborne
satiric
HAMLET................William Shakespeare
"O, what a rogue--"
Director's Note
THE ENTERTAINER............John Osborne
comedy-drama

THE DIRECTOR SPEAKS.... On MEMORIZATION

For One Actress

THE SONG OF BERNADETTE...
Jean and Walter Kerr from
the novel by Franz Werfel
drama-pantomime
AGAMEMNON.....................Aeschylus
high tragedy
EPITAPH FOR GEORGE DILLON...
John Osborne
serious
THE MENAECHMI..................Plautus
comedy

5

THE DIRECTOR SPEAKS...
On VARIETY IN LINE READING

For One Actor and One Actress

THE MOUSE THAT ROARED...
Christopher Sergel from the
book by Leonard Wibberley
comedy
A MAN CALLED PETER......John McGreevey
from the book by
Catherine Marshall
drama
RALLY ROUND THE FLAG, BOYS!...
David Rogers from the
novel by Max Shulman
comedy
PORTRAIT OF JENNIE......Bettye Knapp from
the book by Robert Nathan
romantic

THE DIRECTOR SPEAKS.........On LISTENING

For Two Actors

LUTHER......................John Osborne
drama
EPITAPH FOR GEORGE DILLON...
John Osborne
serious
THE GREAT BIG DOORSTEP...
Frances Goodrich
and Albert Hackett
comedy-dialect
A SOUND OF HUNTING..........Harry Brown
drama

6

THE DIRECTOR SPEAKS... On CONCENTRATION

For Two Actresses

TIGHT LITTLE ISLAND.... Sherman L. Sergel
from the book by Sir Compton MacKenzie
LOOK BACK IN ANGER......... John Osborne
drama
NINE COACHES WAITING.....Guy Bolton from
the novel by Mary Stewart
romantic drama

THE DIRECTOR SPEAKS...
On CHARACTERIZATION

For Three Players

TOM JONES......David Rogers from the novel
by Henry Fielding
(one actor--two actresses).....comedy
SEVEN DAYS IN MAY.... Kristin Sergel based
on the book by Fletcher Knebel
and Charles W. Bailey II
(three actors)................ drama

For Four Players

STARDUST.....................Walter Kerr
(two actors--two actresses)....comedy

For Five Actors

THE BRASS BUTTERFLY.....William Golding
comedy

LIST OF PLAYS

BEFORE THE CURTAIN

I hope you are an adept reader of books--and start with the Preface because it is in these first pages--which are written last--that an author gets to tell you how he feels about his book.

And certainly I want you to know how I feel about this one--for in the pages which follow I think you will find much that is exciting, humorous, dramatic, something of inspiration--and advice which will help you in your study of acting.

Our writers--from Aeschylus to Shulman--which takes us through most of the alphabet--provide a splendid list of scenes. They come from many times and are in wide variety of style and content. I have chosen them for two principal reasons; they are units of drama which, when carefully prepared, will stand as moments of substance and meaning--and the range of styles and emotions will sharpen and develop the player of talent. In some instances you may find your interest in a scene growing until you will want to read and study the full play. This is good and will enrich your concept of character. Any cuts I have made are indicated by a series of dots.

Most importantly this book will give you a chance to act--in scenes ranging from one to four players. Why do I say, "most importantly"? Because after directing thousands of players in nearly three hundred major productions, I have found that the best way for an actor to learn to act is by acting.

You may wonder that I would include what appears to be a cliche in a new work about which

9

I am obviously excited, and yet I chose the phrase
advisedly. It has a new importance as we near the
end of the 1960's for a number of otherwise intelligent theatre people have resuscitated another cliche
which most of us thought had died in the 1930's.
This is the axiom, coined perhaps by David Belasco,
which stated, "The only good actor is the paid actor." In the dawn of this century, when there were
a couple of thousand stock companies across the
land and the most mediocre of plays could tour year
after year, the dictum had some point. The only
actors about were paid and the place of living theatre in the United States was an industry, paying
pleasant dividends, as the Shuberts and Erlangers
would have told you.

The idea that an American citizen could study
theatre in high school and college and later practice
it in his community as a rewarding avocation would
have brought raucous laughter to the lobby of the
Algonquin in the nineteen-teens, had anyone ever
thought of such a ridiculous premise.

The few Broadwayites who could see across
the Hudson in the 1920's must have been amused as
they saw departments of theatre slowly developing
at Iowa, Wisconsin, Carnegie, Northwestern and
other universities and heard that community theatres were developing standards and techniques.

But the laughter in the commercial theatre
silenced rather quickly as the Great Depression
forced a new set of values on the land. With money
almost out of style, the average citizens began to
learn that they could practice the art of theatre,
that the courses in high school and college paid
rich dividends in adult life as they found pleasure
and useful community service in the playhouses of
their towns.

So for the next twenty-five years we gave the

study and practice of theatre more attention--and more participants than had ever been involved actively in an art form in any nation in history. You may recall I said this in 1958 when "The Community Theatre and How It Works" was published. More than eighteen hundred colleges and universities now teach one or more courses in theatre. The number of high schools believing in worthwhile drama to the extent of producing at least one royalty play a year, nears the thirty-thousand mark, and the count of community theatres is still too large a task to achieve accurately. My own estimate is a conservative ten thousand groups of various types.

So this course of the American people finding the same reasons--and like satisfactions--in the practice of theatre which many others know in music, painting, writing, the dance and sculpture-- seemed to be leading quite properly into the new leisure patterns ahead when we will need desperately worthwhile and stimulating activities to fill an increasing number of empty hours.

In the three decades between 1930 and 1960 I would get the occasional question on one of my lecture appearances, "Why doesn't the stock company come back?" My answer was simple: "The taste of those Americans who go to living theatre has so risen, thanks to educational and environmental benefits, that they will no longer accept the artistic faults of the stock company form. A company of fifteen or twenty players cannot possibly be cast correctly for a series of varied plays. The compromises in casting will lead to bad performances and bad productions."

But of late, mirabile dictu, certain Foundations have been pouring millions into revivals of the stock company form--although they paste new labels on the package, such as resident or repertory. So

long as the grants pour in, these groups can oper-
ate but not, apparently, for very long when the
largess languishes. A group on the West Coast
which, in the last decade, received a great fortune
in Foundation grants, announced in July, 1966, that
it was closing. The dispatch said, "With only
$45,000 in gifts guaranteed, it was decided they
could not undertake a season budgeted to cost nearly $500,000." Yes, that's a half million dollars
for one stock company--pardon me, resident company. The director went on to say, "Subsidizing
is absolutely necessary for a community theatre.
Two-thirds of our budget last year was subsidy."

Whether the man chose the wrong term delib-
erately I don't know, but a "community theatre" is
one created by the citizens of a community for the
service of the community. In the ten thousand I
have mentioned, at least ninety-five per cent of the
work is volunteer, a few hundred having trained
professional leadership in the persons of directors,
designers and an occasional business manager.
The great majority present a season of plays in
their towns with a budget of five thousand or less.
A few require more than twenty-five thousand a
year.

Money is notoriously careless about where it
goes but suppose we divided that half million dollar
annual budget, which that California "resident"
company said it had to have, into a hundred parts
and gave five thousand dollars each to a hundred
deserving community playhouses? Can you visual-
ize the improvements possible in equipment and
plants?

But the financial side of our case is far less
important than my concern that actors be allowed
to learn their craft by acting. I suppose some of
the reasons for the millions given to the modern

version of the stock company was to relieve the unemployment among those who would act in New York. I trust you noticed I did not say "Broadway actors" since, unfortunately, so few ever enjoy that pleasure.

When Ralph Bellamy, that fine and talented man, was President of Actors Equity he announced one year that there were twelve hundred new holders of Equity cards; and, said Ralph, "I fear it means twelve hundred more broken hearts." For, you see, of the some twelve thousand holders of Equity cards the unemployment rate varies but slightly from season to season; a range of ninety-two to ninety-four per cent.

So with some twenty "resident" companies now surviving by the grace of subsidy, and paying perhaps an average of twenty actors, we find the Equity unemployment problem, not to mention an equally frightening situation among Los Angeles' Screen Actors Guild, relieved by three per cent! At a cost of how many millions?

Even in our Affluent Society this kind of price tag on a living actor is far too high to be borne by hundreds of cities and towns. This confirms a long-established conclusion of mine that for now, and the foreseeable future, most of our live acting will have to be done by volunteers.

This may be sad news to Belasco's ghost, but then he's not around for the banquet of theatre fare which is enjoyed in every one of our fifty states. The non-commercial actors are hard at work, and they have long been learning to act by acting. Upon the strengthening foundation provided by the educational theatre, play-makers and play-viewers are increasing in number and abilities. Many community theatres are now in their third, fourth and even fifth decades of successful operation. Americans

like to do things well and theatre participants are
no exception. They enjoy so many advantages over
their fellows of the commercial theatre. They are
citizens with jobs, homes and families. They find
in theatre an avocation of challenge and high reward.
They work with sound plays, free from the Broadway fear of the sudden Closing Night. The number
of qualified directors has risen slowly, but fast
enough to make the rise in acting competence fairly
common.

For the Shreveport Little Theatre, 1966-67 is
the Forty-Fifth Consecutive Season. Margaret
Mary Young, with her "Lagniappe" Series, and I,
with the Membership Series, use more than a hundred different players a season in the nine productions. Each year we bring in twenty or thirty new
actors of promise, so there is new vitality coming
always to the acting group. Of our veterans, some
have played with us ten, twenty--and, in one case,
thirty--years. To have apt pupils so long under our
teaching system has given us a performance level
of high quality. Not long ago I told a number of
these veterans, "In the last fifteen seasons each of
you has enjoyed the privilege of playing a greater
number of important roles than any star, man or
woman, has done on Broadway. When I say you do
good work--I mean it. You have learned to act by
acting!"

So then for you I wish the joy of acting--and
that the pages ahead, if you use them well, will increase your techniques, your knowledge--and your
appreciation of theatre.

I used a phrase in Directing the Play from
Selection to Opening Night to describe man's most
human art: "It has the width of imagination, the
length of human experience, and the height of creative expression."

This is the Youngs' feeling about Theatre--we hope it will be yours. Enjoy the book in good health!

JOHN WRAY YOUNG

Shreveport, Louisiana
August 1966

LOOK BACK IN ANGER

by

John Osborne

JIMMY PORTER is a tall, thin young man about twenty-five. He is a disconcerting mixture of sincerity and cheerful malice, of tenderness and freebooting cruelty. He is restless, importunate, full of pride, a combination which alienates the sensitive and insensitive alike. Blistering honesty, or apparent honesty, like his makes few friends. To many he may seem sensitive to the point of vulgarity. To others, he is simply a loudmouth. To be as vehement as he is, is to be almost noncommittal.

The scene is the Porters' shabby one-room flat in a large town in the Midlands of England.

JIMMY

(He moves slowly toward the imagined girl in the chair)

Helena, have you ever watched somebody die? . . . I hope you won't make the mistake of thinking for one moment that I am a gentleman. . . . If you slap my face--by God, I'll lay you out! . . . I'm the type that detests physical violence. Which is why, if I find some woman trying to cash in on what she thinks is my defenseless chivalry by lashing out with her frail little fists, I lash back at her. . . . But you haven't answered my question. I said: have you ever watched somebody die? . . . Anyone who's never watched somebody die is suffering from a pretty bad case of virginity.

(He begins to remember)

17

For twelve months I watched my father dying--
when I was ten years old. He'd come back from
the war in Spain, you see. And certain God-fear-
ing gentlemen there had made such a mess of him,
he didn't have long left to live. Everyone knew it.
Even I knew it.
(He moves R)
But, you see, I was the only one who cared.
(Turns to window. Looking out)
As for my mother, all she could think about was
the fact that she had allied herself to a man who
seemed to be on the wrong side in all things. My
mother was all for being associated with minorities,
provided they were the smart, fashionable ones.
(Moves up C again)
We all of us waited for him to die. The family sent
him a check every month, and hoped he'd get on
with it quietly, without too much vulgar fuss.
(With a kind of appeal in his voice)
But I was the only one who cared.
(He moves L behind the armchair)
Every time I sat on the edge of his bed, to listen
to him talking or reading to me, I had to fight back
my tears. At the end of twelve months, I was the
veteran.
(He leans forward on the back of the armchair)
He would talk to me for hours, pouring out all that
was left of his life to one lonely, bewildered little
boy, who could barely understand half of what he
said. All he could feel was the despair and the
bitterness, the sweet, sickly smell of a dying man.
You see, I learnt at an early age what it was to be
angry--angry and helpless. And I can never forget
it.
(Sits)
I knew more about--love . . . betrayal . . . and
death, when I was ten years old than you will prob-

ably ever know all your life. . . .

(Almost whispering)

Does it matter to you--what people do to me? What
are you trying to do to me?

(Hardly able to get his words out)

My heart is so full, I feel ill--and she wants peace!

(JIMMY has recovered slightly, and manages
to sound almost detached)

I rage, and shout my head off, and everyone thinks:
"Poor chap!" or "What an objectionable young
man!" But that girl there can twist your arm off
with her silence. I've sat in this chair in the dark
for hours. And, although she's known I'm feeling
as I feel now, she's turned over and gone to sleep.
One of us is crazy. One of us is mean and stupid
and crazy. Which is it? Is it me? Is it me, standing here like an hysterical girl, hardly able to get
my words out? Or is it her? Sitting there, putting
on her shoes to go out with that----

(But inspiration has deserted him by now)

Which is it? I wish to heaven you'd try loving her,
that's all. Perhaps, one day, you may want to
come back. I shall wait for that day. I want to
stand up in your tears, and splash about in them,
and sing. I want to be there when you grovel. I
want to be there, I want to watch it, I want the front
seat.

CYRANO DE BERGERAC

by

Edmond Rostand

CYRANO, one of the great characters of all dramatic literature, is famed for his monstrous nose. In this scene he has just been twitted about that feature by a bored young noble looking for a bit of sport. CYRANO, of course, gives the young man much more than he bargained for. The innocent remark which starts the tirade is "You--your nose is--nose is--very large."

CYRANO

No, young man.
That is somewhat too brief. You might say--
   Lord!--
Many and many a thing, changing your tone,
As for example these:--Aggressively:
"Sir, had I such a nose I'd cut it off!"
Friendly: "But it must dip into your cup.
You should have made a goblet tall to drink from."
Descriptive: "'Tis a crag--a peak--a cape!
I said a cape?--'tis a peninsula."
Inquisitive: "To what use do you put
This oblong sheath; is it a writing-case
Or scissors-box?" Or, in a gracious tone:
"Are you so fond of birds, that like a father
You spend your time and thought to offer them
This roosting-place to rest their little feet?"
Quarrelsome: "Well, sir, when you smoke your
   pipe
Can the smoke issue from your nose, without
Some neighbor crying, 'the chimney is afire'?"

20

Warning: "Be careful, lest this weight drag down
Your head, and stretch you prostrate on the ground."
Tenderly: "Have a small umbrella made,
For fear its color fade out in the sun."
Pedantic: "Sir, only the animal
Called by the poet Aristophanes
'Hippocampelephantocámelos'
Should carry so much flesh and bone upon him!"
Cavalier: "Friend, is this peg in the fashion?
To hang one's hat on, it must be convenient."
Emphatic: "Magisterial nose, no wind
Could give thee all a cold, except the mistral."
Dramatic: "'Tis the Red Sea when it bleeds!"
Admiring: "What a sign for a perfumer!"
Poetic: "Is't a conch; are you a Triton?"
Naive: "When does one visit this great sight?"
Respectful: "Let me, sir, pay my respects.
This might be called fronting upon the street."
Countrified: "That's a nose that is a nose!
A giant turnip or a baby melon!"
Or military: "Guard against cavalry!"
Practical: "Will you put it in a raffle?
It surely, sir, would be the winning number!"
Or parodying Pyramus, with a sob:
"There is the nose that ruins the symmetry
Of its master's features; the traitor blushes for it."
My friend, that is about what you'd have said
If you had had some learning or some wit:
But wit, oh! most forlorn of human creatures,
You never had a bit of; as for letters
You only have the four that spell out "Fool"!
Moreover, had you owned the imagination
Needed to give you power, before this hall,
To offer me these mad jests--all of them--
You would not even have pronounced the quarter
O' the half of one's beginning, for I myself
Offer them to myself with dash enough,
But suffer no one else to say them to me.

LUTHER

by

John Osborne

JOHN TETZEL is the colorful and bullying indulgence-vendor. It is 1517 as he enters the market place of Jütebog. He is followed by assistants carrying the banners of the Pope, various religious paraphernalia and a trunk. TETZEL addresses the audience with all the skill of a medicine-show huckster.

TETZEL

Are you wondering who I am, or what I am? Is there anyone here among you, any small child, any cripple, or any sick idiot who hasn't heard of me, and doesn't know why I am here? No? No? Well, speak up then if there is? What, no one? Do you all know me then? Do you all know who I am? If it's true, it's very good, and just as it should be. Just as it should be, and no more than that! However--just in case, mind, there is one blind, maimed midget among you today who can't hear, I will open his ears and wash them out with sacred soap! And, as for the rest of you. I know I can rely on you all to listen patiently while I instruct him. Is that right? Can I go on? I'm asking you, is that right, can I go one? I say "can I go on"?
(Pause)
Thank you. And what is there to tell this blind, maimed midget down there somewhere among you? No, don't look 'round for him, you'll only scare him and then he'll lose his one great chance, and it's not likely to come again, or if it does come,

22

maybe it'll be too late. Well, what's the good news
on this bright day? What's the information you
want? It's this! Who is this friar with his red
cross? Who sent him and what's he here for? No!
Don't try to work it out for yourself, because I'm
going to tell you now, this very minute. I am John
Tetzel, Dominican, inquisitor, sub-commissioner
to the archbishop of Mainz, and what I bring you
is indulgences. Indulgences made possible by the
red blood of Jesus Christ, and the red cross you
see standing up here behind me is the standard of
those who carry them. Look at it! Take a good
look at it! What else do you see up there? Well,
what do they look like? Why, it's the arms of his
holiness, because why? Because it's him who sent
me here. Yes, my friend, the Pope himself has
sent me with indulgences for you! Fine, you say,
but what are indulgences? And what are they to
me? What are indulgences? They're only the most
precious and noble of God's gifts to men, that's all
they are! Before God, I tell you I wouldn't swap
my privilege at this moment with that of St. Peter
in Heaven, because I've already saved more souls
with my indulgences than he could ever have done
with all his sermons. You think that's bragging,
do you? Well, listen a little more carefully, my
friend, because this concerns you! Just look at it
this way. For every mortal sin you commit, the
Church says that after confession and contrition,
you've got to do penance--either in this life or in
purgatory--for seven years. Seven years! Right?
Are you with me? Good. Now then, how many
mortal sins are committed by you--by you--in a
single day? Just think for one moment; in one
single day of your life. Can you find the answer?
Oh, not so much as one a day. Very well then,
how many in a month? How many in six months?

How many in a year? And how many in a whole
lifetime? Yes, you needn't fidget in your seat--it
doesn't bear thinking about, does it? Try and add
up all the years of torment piling up! What about
it? And isn't there anything you can do about this
terrible situation you're in? Do you really want
to know? Yes! There is something, and that something I have here with me today: letters, letters of
indulgence. Hold up the letters so that everyone
can see them. Look at them, all properly sealed,
an indulgence in every envelope, and one of them
can be yours today, now, before it's too late! Look
at them! Take a good look. There isn't any one sin
so big that one of these letters can't remit it. I
challenge anyone here, any member of this audience,
to present me with a sin, anything, any kind of a
sin, I don't care what it is, that I can't settle for
him with one of these precious little envelopes.
Why, if anyone had ever offered violence to the
blessed Virgin Mary, Mother of God, if he'd only
pay up--as long as he paid up all he could--he'd
find himself forgiven. You think I'm exaggerating?
You do, do you? Well, I'm authorized to go even
further than that. Not only am I empowered to give
you these letters of pardon for the sins you've already committed, I can pardon you for those sins
you haven't even committed.
    (Pause . . . then slowly)
But, which, however, you intend to commit! But,
you ask--and it's a fair question--why is our Holy
Lord prepared to distribute such a rich grace to
me? The answer, my friends, is all too simple.
It's so that we can restore the ruined church of St.
Peter and St. Paul in Rome! So that it won't have
its equal anywhere in the world. This great church
contains the bodies not only of the holy apostles
Peter and Paul, but of a hundred thousand martyrs

and no less than forty-six popes! To say nothing
of the relics like St. Veronica's handkerchief, the
burning bush of Moses and the very rope with which
Judas Iscariot hanged himself! But, alas, my
friends, this fine old building is threatened with
destruction, and all these things with it, unless a
sufficient restoration fund is raised, and raised
soon.

(With passionate irony)

. . . Will anyone dare to say that the cause is not
a good one?

(Pause)

. . . So won't you, for as little as one quarter of
a florin, my friend, buy yourself one of these letters, so that in the hour of death, the gate of paradise be flung open for you? And, these letters
aren't just for the living, but for the dead, too.
There can't be one amongst you who hasn't at least
one dear one who has departed--and to who knows
what? So don't hold back; come forward, think of
your dear ones, think of yourselves! For twelve
groats, or whatever it is we think you can afford,
you can rescue your father from agony and yourself
from certain disaster. And if you only have the
coat on your back, then strip it off, strip it off now
so that you can obtain grace. For remember: As
soon as your money rattles in the box and the cash
bell rings, the soul flies out of purgatory and sings!
So, come on, then. Get your money out! What is
it, have your wits flown away with your faith? Listen, soon, I shall take down the cross, shut the
gates of heaven, and put out the brightness of this
sun of grace that shines on you here today.

(He flings a large coin into the open strongbox,
where it rattles furiously)

The Lord our God reigns no longer. He has re-
signed all power to the Pope. In the name of the

Father, and of the Son and of the Holy Ghost. Amen.
In the name of the Father, and of the Son and of the
Holy Ghost. Amen. In the name of the Father, and
of the Son and of the Holy Ghost. Amen.

    (The sound of coins clattering like rain into a
    great coffer as the light fades)

NOTE: TETZEL is a fascinating character: shrewd,
    calculating, and a bit greedy. In the Broadway
    production he was played in the manner of the
    pitchman at the fair, selling his do-it-all veg-
    etable slicer to any and all customers. There
    was even a touch of Brooklyn accent in that per-
    formance. You can play him in other ways;
    perhaps as the over-zealous do-gooder who
    meant well in the beginning but has been car-
    ried far afield, mayhap by the fascination of
    his own voice.

HAMLET

by

William Shakespeare

HAMLET, by some considered the mightiest role ever written for the stage, is a man of emotions so varied and intense that an actor is presented with exciting challenges within a single speech. In Act II, Scene Two, HAMLET is searching for a way to avenge his father and bring his uncle to justice. For people of theatre this speech is particularly attractive since in it HAMLET considers, and decides, that the play is the device he needs. Polonius and the Players have just left him.

HAMLET

O, what a rogue and peasant slave am I!
Is it not monstrous that this player here,
But in a fiction, in a dream of passion,
Could force his soul so to his own conceit
That from her working all his visage wann'd,
Tears in his eyes, distraction in's aspect,
A broken voice, and his whole function suiting
With forms to his conceit? And all for nothing!
For Hecuba!
What's Hecuba to him, or he to Hecuba,
That he should weep for her? What would he do,
Had he the motive and the cue for passion
That I have? He would drown the stage with tears,
And cleave the general ear with horrid speech,
Make mad the guilty, and appall the free,
Confound the ignorant, and amaze, indeed,
The very faculties of eyes and ears.
Yet I,

A dull and muddy-mettled rascal, peak,
Like John-a-dreams, unpregnant of my cause,
And can say nothing; no, not for a king
Upon whose property and most dear life
A damn'd defeat was made.   Am I a coward?
Who calls me villain? breaks my pate across?
Plucks off my beard, and blows it in my face?
Tweaks me by the nose? gives me the lie i' the
          throat,
As deep as to the lungs? who does me this, Ha!
'Swounds, I should take it: for it cannot be
But I am pigeon-liver'd, and lack gall
To make oppression bitter; or ere this
I should have fatted all the region kites
With this slave's offal: Bloody, bawdy villain!
Remorseless, treacherous, lecherous, kindless
          villain!
Oh, vengeance!
Why, what an ass am I! This is most brave,
That I, the son of a dear father murder'd,
Prompted to my revenge by heaven and hell,
Must, like a whore, unpack my heart with words,
And fall a-cursing like a very drab,
A scullion!
Fie upon't! foh!--About, my brain! I have heard
That guilty creatures, sitting at a play,
Have by the very cunning of the scene
Been struck so to the soul that presently
They have proclaim'd their malefactions;
For murder, though it have no tongue, will speak
With most miraculous organ. I'll have these
          players
Play something like the murder of my father
Before mine uncle; I'll observe his looks;
I'll tent him to the quick; if he but blench,
I know my course. The spirit that I have seen
May be the devil: and the devil hath power

To assume a pleasing shape; yea, and perhaps
Out of my weakness and my melancholy,
As he is very potent with such spirits,
Abuses me to damn me; I'll have grounds
More relative than this--the play's the thing
Wherein I'll catch the conscience of the king.

THE DIRECTOR SPEAKS

I think the centuries have proved that there is
no one right way to play Hamlet. The tremendous
role has been assayed by young, mature, middle-
aged and old men and, upon rare occasion, by wom-
en.   Until the last few decades most great male
stars of the theatre felt that performance of the
Dane should be the apogee of their careers. Some
of the virtuoso actors played the role for so many
years that they themselves grew from young men
to old.

So, it seems to me, there is great freedom in
approaching this scene.   There have been those
who have felt that Hamlet could not really be a
young man for his knowledge, his words, his wit
implied many years of living. This, I fear, betrays
a lack of understanding the relationship between
the mind of a character and that of his creator, the
playwright.

Shakespeare's people share in common the beautiful mental agility and unique vocabulary which
were major elements of his genius.   This should
not awe us but rather make us glad that, in approaching a Shakespearean character, we have so much on
our side.   As we move into the thought processes
and the emotional transitions, we may find our-

selves beginning to create a character which thinks
in a Shakespearean manner. This tenuous and difficult task of finding and adopting the thought pattern is important in approaching the work of playwrights all the way from Aeschylus to Osborne.

So choose your own approach to Hamlet. Concentrate upon the _meaning_ of the words--their
beauty will take care of itself. I like it that this
speech is so concerned with the _play_ as a device.

THE ENTERTAINER
by
John Osborne

Archie Rice is a product of the cheapest of the English variety theatre. His father a performer before him, Archie has lived in a world of vulgarity breathing an atmosphere which has always been filled with the newest--and worst--music.

Archie is about fifty. He has a slight stoop, from a kind of inverted pedantry which he original- ly assumed thirty years ago when he left one of London's minor public day schools. Landladies adore him because he is so friendly, and obviously such a gentleman. Some of his fellow artists even call him "Professor" occasionally, as they might call a retired Army Captain "Colonel." He smiles kindly at this simplicity, knowing himself to belong to no class, and plays the part as well as he knows how.

Mr. Osborne regrets the passing of the music hall for he feels that with it goes a significant part of England . . . something that once belonged to everyone.

In this, the final scene of "The Entertainer," the actor has opportunity to bring out the larger- than-life values as Archie goes through his last performance on the dingy music hall stage, with the nude tableau drop behind him.

ARCHIE

I've just come to tell you about the wife. She's gone back to her husband. She has, straight. Don't clap too hard, we're all in a very old building. Yes,

31

very old. Old. What about that? What about her,
oh--madam with the helmet on? I reckon she's sag-
ging a bit, if you ask me. She needs some beef
putting into her--the roast beef of Old England. No,
nobody's asking me, never mind. Nice couple of
fried eggs, anyway. She's a nice girl, though--
a nice girl. Going steady with Charlie here--isn't
she, Charlie?

(To the conductor.)

She met him in a revolving door and they've been
going around together ever since. I'm doing me nut,
you know that, don't you? I'm doing me nut up here.
Nudes, that's what they call them, lady, nudes.
Blimey, she's got more clothes on than I have. It's
a lot of madam, that's all it is. A lot of madam.
Oh, I put a line in there. Never mind, it doesn't
matter. I've made a few tumbles in my time. I
have, honest. You wouldn't think I was sexy to look
at me, would you? No, honestly, you wouldn't,
would you, lady? I always reckon you feel stronger after it.

(Sings.)

"Say your jelly-roll is fine, but it don't compare
with mine!" There's a bloke at the side here with
a hook, you know that, don't you? He is, he's
standing there. I can see him. Must be the income
tax man. Life's funny though, isn't it? It is--life's
funny. It's like sucking a sweet with the wrapper
on. Oh, well, we're all in the fertilizer business
now, I suppose. Well, I'd rather have a glass of
beer any day--I would. You don't believe me, but
I would. You think I'm gone, don't you? Go on,
say it, you think I'm gone. You think I'm gone,
don't you? Well, I am. What's the matter, you
feeling cold up there? Before I do go, ladies and
gentlemen, I should just like to tell you a little
story, a little story. This story is about a man,

just a little, ordinary man, like you and me, and
one day he woke up and found himself in paradise.
Well, he looks up, you see, and he sees a feller
standing next to him. It turns out that this feller
is a saint or something. Anyway, he's on the welcoming committee. And the feller says to him--
the Saint--says to him; "Well," he says, "you're
now in paradise." "Am I?" he says, "You are,"
says the Saint, "What's more, you have earned
yourself eternal happiness." "Have I?" he says.
"You most certainly have," says the Saint. "Oh,
you're well away," he says. "Can't you hear the
multitudes? Why, everyone is singing, everyone
is joyful. What do you say, my son?" So the little
man took a look around him at all the multitudes of
the earth, spread out against the universe. So he
says to the Saint: "Well, can I get up where you're
standing, and take a proper look?" So the Saint
says: "Of course you can, my son," and makes
way for him. And the little man stood up where the
Saint was and gazed up at the sight around him. At
all the Hosts of Heaven, and all the rest of it. "All
the wonder and the joy of eternity is round about
you," said the Saint. "You mean, this is all eternity and I'm in paradise?" "That is so, my son.
Well, what have you to say?" So the little man
looks round again for a bit, and the Saint says; "Well,
my son?" "Well," he says, "I've often wondered
what I'd say if this ever happened to me. I couldn't
think, somehow." And the Saint smiled at him
kindly and says again; "And what do you say, my
son?" "Only one thing I can say," says the little
man.

    (He makes a whistling sound)
Well, the Saint looked as if he had been struck a-
cross the face by some great hand. The Hosts
stopped singing and all the Angels hid their faces,

and for a tiny splash in eternity there was no sound
at all in Paradise. The Saint couldn't speak for a
while, and then he threw his arms round the little
man, and kissed him. And he said: "I love you,
my son. With all my soul I shall love you always.
I have been waiting to hear that ever since I came
here." He's there with his little hook, I can see
him. Oh, well, I have to go, don't I? I have to go.

THE DIRECTOR SPEAKS

on

MEMORIZATION

Too many concerned with acting, and this includes teachers, directors and players, achieve far less than their potential because they fail to give a starting point of technique its proper attention. This, of course, is Memorization--the very first letter of the actor's alphabet.

Modern American life asks little of man's memory. The machines are remembering more and more things for us so that now one who can recall both his Social Security number and that on his car license plate is regarded with awe.

This will not do for the actor. Since, among a number of intricate processes, the craft calls for translation of the printed words of a playwright into audible and visible emotion, it follows that we can translate most effectively only after we have learned the words and they are held in easy command by the memory.

To gain most value from our scenes, then, may I urge you to learn the words so that you can then move on to the higher, and more important, elements of acting.

I have found that many actors who come to work with the Youngs have never been told that Memorization is a three-part process and neglect of any one of the parts impairs and delays the whole.

Everyone understands the first step: learning through the eyes, the lifelong approach to "study" which begins in the first school years. This the actor must do but it is not enough. For any who have come to rehearsal after long eye-study and been puzzled that little seemed learned when cues were spoken--not seen--there is need to realize that the auditory sense is different from the visual. In the theatre cues come to the actor through his ears--not from a printed page--and so he must study the sound of words as someone reads his cues. Even in one-actor scenes a third of study time should be vocalized since the sound of one's own voice is a different sensory experience than that of regarding printed words.

Many actors study both the sight and the sound of lines and still come to rehearsal unprepared because they have not worked in the third division of Memorization--the kinetic sense. Acting is many things, and among the most important is movement. This needs simultaneous study until every gesture, step and piece of business is memorized with the exact word or phrase.

When the player has full command of his role visually, aurally and kinetically, then he is ready to move on to higher, and more difficult, elements of technique. If you will consider the full implication of this statement then you will know why I consider one of the most brutal criticisms in theatre the performance which can bring only the remark, "Well, at least they knew their lines!"

THE SONG OF BERNADETTE

Dramatized by
Jean and Walter Kerr

from the novel by
Franz Werfel

As the Kerrs say of the play, "The most important reality in the action of the play is a spiritual one, and this is best realized by concentrating almost exclusively on those forces which are capable of carrying such action."

The vision of the Lady is done imaginatively, rather than literally. This is an advantage the play has over the motion picture version, since no actress could equal in the audience eye what BERNADETTE sees with hers.

BERNADETTE SOUBIROUS is a simple and not too intelligent child who is possessed of a great love, for which she is willing to fight. She is not a philosopher, nor a deliberate mystic, as many of the Saints have been. She was not, so far as she knew, even particularly "religious." She was ordinary, backward, honest, and lucky. She was <u>chosen.</u>

The scene is the grotto at Massabielle. We are looking out from under the overhanging rock toward the river bank. Her sister, Marie, and a friend, Jeanne Abadie, have gone to look for more firewood.

BERNADETTE

Wait, don't go without me! All right, then, Jeanne Abadie, you're no friend of mine.

(She looks after them, breathing heavily, for
a few moments. Then she turns slowly back
and comes downstage, calmer now)
I didn't mean that. Why should they wait for me?
I'd be no use to them.

(Whipping back suddenly, she cries out loudly)
But I'm not a touchy little runt!

(Turning front again, she moves down left)
I'm the oldest. I should do the most.

(She stands still, debating)
I wouldn't get a cold. Not on account of a little
water.

(Quickly, BERNADETTE sits on the rock down
left and slips off her shoes, then one of her white
woolen stockings. As she begins to remove the
other, she stops suddenly, listening. Music is
heard, faintly at first. BERNADETTE frowns,
and continues to listen. She peers off down
left, as though searching for the music's source,
turns, and crosses slowly toward up right,
still searching and listening. Finally she
stops, her frown deepening thoughtfully. Now
she quickly puts her hands to her cheeks, then
one hand to her forehead, as though afraid she
might have a fever. Dropping her hands, she
shakes her head slightly, as though concluding
that she has no fever. But she makes up her
mind:)
I'd better go home.

(BERNADETTE starts to cross toward the
down left rock, but midway happens to glance
upward into the grotto, right of center. She
stops, thunderstruck. The music reaches a
crescendo. BERNADETTE stands transfixed,
staring up into the grotto, slightly over our
heads and slightly right, for a long moment.
Then, she rubs her eyes, doubting her senses.

But as she opens her eyes again, the same
vivid expression of seeing something above
comes over her face, and her mouth drops
open)

But it's all rock! No one could get up there. . . .

(Slowly, BERNADETTE advances downstage.
When she reaches her final position, she pauses, and then breaks into a great smile, as
though in response to one. She quickly raises
her hand in an awkward gesture of greeting,
but it falters in the act and she lets her hand
drop. Softly, almost breathlessly, eyes shin-
ing, she speaks:)

Oh! . . . How beautiful you are!

(This is held for a moment. Suddenly a look
of apprehension crosses her face and her hands
fly up part way in warning.)

Be careful! You'll fall!

(She takes in a breath sharply, then relaxes,
relieved. She smiles again, not so impulsively, but tenderly)

Who are you?

(She waits for an answer, then shakes her head
in a questioning negative, puzzled, as though
saying "You won't tell me?")

May I stay here with you?

(She pauses, and then inclines her head very
slightly, as though she had received an affirm-
ative nod for an answer. Now, as though without conscious thought, she lowers herself to her
knees, always staring up into the grotto. She
smiles slightly, and seems very happy. After
a moment, she automatically reaches into her
apron pocket and takes out her rosary. Without taking her eyes from the grotto above, she
starts to say her beads very softly)

"Hail Mary, full of grace, the Lord is with thee.

. . . Blessed art thou among women. . . ."
(Bernadette's voice fades to an aspirate and
she mouths the rest of the "Ave." She goes
on to the next bead, repeating the silent words
with her lips)

AGAMEMNON

by

Aeschylus

The AGAMEMNON represents Aeschylus at the height of his lyric and dramatic power. The protagonists are mighty figures swept up in a tempest of passion which comes not from a day but from long ages of hereditary evil. The murder of her husband by CLYTEMNESTRA and her infidelity with Agamemnon's cousin stem from the crime-filled history of the Atreus family. AGAMEMNON is, of course, the first play of the ORESTEIA, Aeschylus' only surviving trilogy and written but two years before his death. It is the great talent at the height of its power. Critics regard the AGAMEMNON as truly sublime--both as drama and poetry.

CLYTEMNESTRA, the evil deeds consummated, gives answer to the angry crowd which demands to know what has happened to their king. The door of the palace swings open and the bodies of Agamemnon and Cassandra lie just within. CLYTEMNESTRA stands over them--blood-stains on her face and dress.

CLYTEMNESTRA

Words, endless words, I spoke to serve my purpose.
Now I gainsay them all and feel no shame.
How can a woman work her hatred out
On him she hates, and yet must seem to love,
how pile up ruin 'round him, fence the snare
too high to leap beyond--except by lies?
Long years ago I planned. Now it is done.
Old hatred ended. It was slow in coming,

but it came--
I stand here where I struck. So did I.
Nothing do I deny. I flung around him
a cloak, full folds, deadly folds. I caught him,
fish in a net. No way to run or fight.
Twice did I strike him and he cried out twice
and his limbs failed him and he fell, and there
I gave him the third stroke, an offering
to the god of hell who holds fast all his dead.
So there he lay and as he gasped, his blood
spouted and splashed me with black spray, a dew
of death, sweet to me as heaven's sweet raindrops
when the corn-land buds.
There stands the matter, ancient men of Argos.
Go now, and if you can, rejoice. For me,
I glory. Oh, if such a thing might be,
over the dead to pour thank-offerings,
over this dead it would be just and more.
So full of curses did he fill the cup
his house drank--but the dregs he drank himself.
Bring me to trial like any silly woman?
My heart is fearless, and you all well know
what I know. Curse me or bless me--either as you
will--
all one to me. Look. This is Agamemnon
my husband, dead, struck down by my right hand,
a righteous workman.
So now do you pass judgment on
me? Exile--
the people's hate--cursed by men openly.
But he--you never spoke a word to cross him,
who cared no more than if a beast should die
when flocks are plenty in the fleecy fold,
and slew his daughter, dearest anguish borne
by me in travail--slew her for a charm
against the Thracian winds. Oh, never
would you drive him away from land and home,

a thing polluted. Now the deed is mine.
You are a stern judge then. I tell you plainly
threaten what threats you will. I am content
that you shall rule if your hand prove the stronger.
But if God please the other way about,
you shall be taught, though late, the ways of wis-
    dom.
The oath I swear is holy.
By justice for my child now consummated,
by black, blind Doom, by all the powers of hell,
to whom I offered what I killed, I swear
hope does not tread the halls of fear for me
while on my hearth a fire is still kindled
by one now true in heart to me as ever,
Aegisthus, my sure shield of confidence.
Here lies the man who scorned me--me, his wife--
the fool and tool of every shameless woman
beneath Troy's walls. Here she lies too, his
    slave.
got by his spear, his sibyl bed-fellow,
his paramour--God's words upon her lips,
who rubbed the galley's benches at his side.
They have their due, he thus and she the same,
her swan-song sung. His lover--there she lies.
I in my soft bed lying, shall delight,
thinking of her, still more in its smooth softness.

EPITAPH FOR GEORGE DILLON

by

John Osborne and Anthony Creighton

RUTH is about forty, slim and attractive. She has come from work but her clothes are attractive. A package has arrived from Jock returning a watch she had given him, and a farewell letter. In her hurt and bitterness she speaks to a Jock she imagines sitting before her. To her right is a small table, on it a typewriter, and behind this a chair. She turns suddenly to face the table.

RUTH

Reasons! What the hell's the use of giving reasons. You'll find reasons of your own anyway. I'm going, it's all over, kaput, finished! What is it Josie says? "You've had your lot!" That's all there is to it. You've had your lot! It's not very pleasant, is it? The heart of the matter, in a neat, trivial, nasty little phrase. You can't escape from it--it's the voice of the world, Jock. Listen to it. You can't go on closing your ears to it forever. It isn't a nice, gentle, modulated voice. I know: I live with it every day of my life. Open your ears--nobody gives a damn about you. You've had your lot! You've been a promising young man for too long. Youthful promise doesn't look too well with receding hair after a while. God, no! Not tears, Jock --not that now. You must want me to despise you very much--well, you're succeeding. You're determined to run the whole disgusting gamut, aren't you? The complete flop. All right then, let's make sure of it, if that's how you really want it. You want a specific reason for my walking out on you, no matter how meaningless, no matter how idiotic. Well, here it is: you told me you hadn't a penny, not even the price of a packet of cigarettes, you said. Do you know what I did? I did an inexcusable thing. I went to your jacket pocket when you were downstairs. Something made me do it. And inside, I find a check for eight guineas for some review or other that you'd written. You hadn't even told me it had been accepted. I suppose it's unsigned, as usual. Not only did you lie about the money, but you even kept your piffling little success from me. A brainless, cheap little lie. And that did it--the whole works collapsed, the whole flimsy works. Does that satisfy you? Well, does it? Is that pointless enough for you? You've made me sound like a first-class bitch, and I've given you a first-class bitchy reason. It's all wrapped up for you--take it with both hands.

(Leaning over the table)

Oh, Jock--I've tried. I really have tried. I can't go on, saying the same things to you.

(Moves up, facing upstage)

I shall go mad. Just look at us now; we've had this same scene so many times before. I feel sick, standing here, listening to it. The same dialogue, the same words even, the particular words, your favorite expressions and mine; me looking out of this damned window forever, and you sitting with your head in your hands. We can't even bear to look at each other. I can look out on that street, and see the setting of every line on your face. I've got to be ruthless. With myself.

(Turns and moves down to table)

Come on, we'll have a fag, anyway. No, keep yours.

(Throws packet into darkness)

Last two.

(Lights up)

I must sit down a moment.

　　(She sits at the table, stares across it, then
　　slips something beneath the typewriter)

You've got a little patch of gray behind your ear.
I've only just noticed it. . . . I'll have to go now,
Jock.

　　(Rising to L)

I've spent nearly six years, giving all I could to
you, giving you belief in yourself, giving my love
--such as it is. All that--washing out your shirts;
making sure you changed your socks regularly; trying to hide the cigarette burns you leave all over
the place; keeping that gas ring, that you manage
to make so disgusting, from making the place smell
uninhabitable; making love to you in between the odd,
snatched comforts, the cigarettes and the bottle of
beer. All that was simply a part of it. I did make
you believe in yourself, didn't I? I have given you
that, Jock. For six years. It doesn't cancel out
simply because I'm no longer coming around here
twice a week. It hasn't been for nothing.

　　(To table)

It can't have been, surely. Oh, why should I be
made to feel so shoddy and futile! It's you--sitting
there, making a wax image of every word I utter.
What's the use!

　　(Fingering the table)

You've burnt this table again. . . . I suppose at
any moment that seedy little man will ring the bell
downstairs, and come up here to stand at the door,
all leers and triumph, asking you for his rent, and
mentally undressing me at the same time. It'll be
sordid, and you'll sit there, helpless, loathing him
and loathing me. I shall even have to pay him his
rent in front of you. I'm still too much of a novice
not to have given it to you in advance. Your humil-

iation really does seem to be the breath of life to
everyone around you, doesn't it? Well, I'm not
going to take part in it any longer. By the way,
there's still some tea and a few tins of stuff in the
cupboard for you. Where did I put my case?

(RUTH has put on her coat, carries her hat,
   and stands L, with her case beside her)
Good-by, Jock. I shall be forty-one on Monday.
Do you remember? We were going out. Or, as
you'd hasten to point out, I was going to take you
out. I wonder where we'd have gone. A rather
arty film somewhere, I expect. Then the pub, and
back here. . . . Think of this, as just another unimportant rejection slip for your collection. Put
it with the others. Only for heaven's sake, don't
put a hand out to me now.

(Picks up case)
We both deserve something better. What was it all
for?

THE MENAECHMI

by

Plautus

Titus Maccius Plautus, the first important writer of Roman comedy, lived from about 254--historians are uncertain of his birth date--until 184 B.C. His early life was rugged, and perhaps rather bawdy, characteristics prominent in many of his plays. He was soldier, baker's assistant and actor, in that he played the Maccus, the standard clown's role.

He was about fifty when he decided to become a playwright and his hard-won knowledge of common Roman life and his experience in the popular show-manship of the day stood him in good stead. He wrote some one hundred and thirty plays, from which twenty-one are extant.

His work influenced playwrights of later ages but perhaps his most frequently imitated farce is THE MENAECHMI, which deals in depth with nearly all the comic possibilities of identical twins. Sixteen centuries later Mr. Shakespeare adapted the play into one of his successes called "The Comedy of Errors," and in the Twentieth Century Rogers and Hart adapted Shakespeare's adaptation and it became "The Boys from Syracuse."

EROTIUM, the courtesan, deals delightfully in the lusty humor of the early version of La Dolce Vita! She is the mistress of one of the twins, Menaechmi of Epidamnus. She has charm and vitality.

EROTIUM

(Enters and speaks to her servants within)

Leave the door thus: I would not have it shut:

Begone: make ready: see that ev'rything
Be done that's wanting; lay the couches smooth,
Let the perfumes be set on fire. 'Tis neatness
Lures the fond lover's heart. A spruce appearance
Is damage to the lover, gain to us.
But where, where is he, whom the cook inform'd
    me
Was at the door? I see him, he's a gentleman,
from whom I draw much service and much profit;
And therefore I'm content, that he should hold,
As he deserves, with me, the highest place.
I'll go and speak to him. My life! my soul!
I marvel you should stand here at the door,
That's open to you more than is your own;
Your own it is. - Sweet, ev'rything is ready
Which you desir'd: nothing to stay you, love:
The dinner, which you order'd, we have got:
Then, whensoe'er you please, you may sit down. . . .
'Tis Venus' will
I should prefer you before all my lovers:
Nor on your part unmerited for you
You only with your gifts enrich me. . . .
But prithee, sweet, come in: 'twere better for
    you. . . .
Let's in to dinner. . . .
Why did you bid me then to get a dinner? . . .
For you and your parasite. . . .
The parasite; in other words, the Dishcloth. . . .
He, I say,
Who came with you this morning, when you brought
    me
The robe that you had stolen from your wife. . . .
Why are you pleas'd to hold me for your sport?
And why do you deny what you have done? . . .
Given me a robe belonging to your wife. . . .
I prithee, now have done
With jesting thus, and come along with me. . . .

But do you know, sweet, what I'd have you do? . . .
The robe you gave me
I'd have you carry it to the embroiderer's,
To be made up anew; with such additions,
As I shall order,
So then by and by,
Sweet, you shall take it with you, when you go. . . .
Let's in now.

THE DIRECTOR SPEAKS

on

VARIETY IN LINE READING

A vital element of acting technique which lends itself admirably to your work with these scenes is that of variety in reading lines. Proficiency can make a fair actor sound good; lack of variety can make a talented actor far less than he should be.

Again, as with listening and projection, variety in speech runs counter to a number of today's environmental pressures. Speed is accepted by most as an essential of American life, leading, at times, to a confusion of hurry and rush with efficiency. The monosyllabic vocabulary, the one-note voice: these are among the facts of life in our time and the actor has to acknowledge them--but he must make certain they do not impair his work on the stage.

For a simple and direct approach to improving the actor's variety, I like to divide the subject into four general headings. The first of these is Variety of Time.

While most Americans lack variety in their time-rate, it's misuse is far too flagrant among those who should know better. Did you ever have a teacher, whose material might have been excellent but whose steady, monotonous rate led toward hypnosis rather than learning? Have you ever heard a political speech, filled though it may have been with the most noble sentiments, which came through in delivery with all the persuasion and effectiveness of a steady drip of water from a leaky tap? I was going to ask if you'd ever listened to a sermon, from which you expected so much, only to find the regular pulsation of the droning voice evoking little but a desire for slumber--but then perhaps you've been more fortunate than I.

This fault, then, the actor cannot allow himself. Since the larger part of a play's impact comes from the constantly varied stream of aural stimuli --as actors transmit playwrights' words--anything less than the most effective transmission is not enough. If you want a quick example of the gain for the actor by improving Variety of Time, do one of these scenes on a tape recorder keeping the speech rate as steady as you possibly can. Then do the same scene with this simple change: Give more time to the important words and phrases-- and less time to the less important. Record it-- and now listen to both. Beyond this simple beginning lies the infinite variety of time which, brought to a high level, will increase the actor's efficiency in his important mission of transmitting thoughts and emotions through the sound of words.

Second, on my list, is Variety of Pitch, again a speech element opposed to the general pattern of American speech. For all our melting-pot heritage it is almost strange that we did not carry into our speech the many-note, lilting or even violent qualities of British, Italian, Irish, Spanish and other national speech patterns.

But these past two centuries have been busy ones for us and it may be more efficient to say "Good morning, how are you?" on a single note than to take the time to wander up and down the scale as in some other languages. But, again, the actor cannot afford this easy way, unless he is playing a gangster--or, mayhap, a cowboy.

The additional stimuli which come from excellent use of a voice of wide range are tools which good players need--and can acquire. Millions found Sir John Gielgud's "Ages of Man" a television delight. One of Sir John's best tools is his Variety of Pitch.

Listening to recordings by great actors will illustrate the values of widened pitch range. Simple exercises, such as counting from one to ten--starting on your lowest note and ascending to a comfortable high--is helpful. Portions of the alphabet may be used, and I think you will find that a few weeks of practice will bring some command of more notes in your speaking voice.

There is no simple rule for using this ability but you will find, as you work toward the best possible readings, that the added color and interest in your voice will make you a more effective transmitter of thought and emotion--and that is one of our major objectives.

Variety of Volume is probably less neglected than Time and Pitch, and yet many players are guilty of its underuse. In real life we do a fair job of increasing volume in moments of violent emotional content and decreasing it when we are conveying tenderness or sadness. The most difficult problem in teaching proper use of volume lies in the beginning actor who is so often "afraid I'll be too loud." Unaccustomed to the decibel level of proper stage speech, the shy beginner should attend performances by the greatest actors of our day and listen to the strong voice take command, impose attention on an audience, and work never below complete audibility. While a whisper can be as dramatic as any voice-use in theatre, the whisper is not that used in a living room--it has to be produced with projection sufficient to carry to the spectators in the last row.

A simple program to build strength in your voice: five minutes of deep breathing, preferably

as you walk, and ten minutes of closing yourself
in a room and reading aloud--at full voice--any
material you choose. Don't strain--but at the end
of each week you should find your voice gaining
strength and size.

The fourth Variety is that of Energy--or Emo-
tion--for the actor the terms are interlocked. Most
complex of our series, this quality is present in all
good performances, for its lack leaves little but a
dullness and grayness of sound from a player even
though varieties of Time, Pitch and Volume are
well used.

Part of characterization growth, this variety
evolves from careful study of meanings and emotional values. It is not a surface process but does
require careful analysis of outer manifestations to
make certain that they are projecting accurately
the inner emotion.

This is intimately related to one of the stage's
old axioms: "Good acting comes from within."
There is no simple route to exact use of Variety
of Energy. It is one of the techniques which need
study, experience--and time. I think you may be
able to check your own progress by going back to
some of these scenes after three or four months--
prepare them again. The surface elements will
return quickly, but see if perhaps the emotional values and your projection of them have not become
more three-dimensional, richer, more effective.
If you can report such progress--you are truly developing as a player.

THE MOUSE THAT ROARED

by

Christopher Sergel

from the book by

Leonard Wibberly

GLORIANA THE TWELFTH is a stunning girl in her twenties who walks with a stately air. As sovereign of Grand Fenwick, her first concern is for her tiny country, but the conflict with the United States is far from her liking. She is ready for advice from her uncle.

COUNT MOUNTJOY, the uncle, is an aristocrat and leader of Grand Fenwick's Anti-Dilutionist Party. He is a wise politician and knows that even though Grand Fenwick now has a Q-Bomb, it is not the way to peace. MOUNTJOY is on stage as GLORIANA enters.

MOUNTJOY

Remember the motto of the Mountjoy family: Defend the Duchy through Statecraft.

GLORIANA

(As she crosses)
What about your family?

MOUNTJOY

My dearest wish is that we should continue to serve the descendants of Sir Roger for all time. But this may not come to pass.

GLORIANA

You're going away?

MOUNTJOY

No, your Grace. I refer to the possibility there may be no descendants to serve.

GLORIANA

Why not?

MOUNTJOY

To come directly to the point, your Grace is un-married. . . . The royal line of Fenwick is in danger of extinction.

GLORIANA

I can't be thinking of marriage in a time of crisis.

MOUNTJOY

That's the time you should think of it.

GLORIANA
(Smiling uneasily as she touches the scarf which she's wearing)
I'm not sure I'd want to marry. Certainly I won't marry someone just because you feel it has political advantages.

MOUNTJOY

You hold the destiny of a people in your hands, Gloriana. Your marriage has to serve their interests.

GLORIANA
(Clutching the scarf now)
That's old-fashioned nonsense. I don't care to discuss it further.

MOUNTJOY

The matter is much too vital for anything as unpredictable as personal affection.

GLORIANA
I won't go into this, Uncle.

MOUNTJOY
(Pressing)
It may affect the internal security of the realm!

GLORIANA
(Puzzled)
How could marrying some bloodline affect our security?

MOUNTJOY
The matter is much more urgent than you realize.
(In her agitation, GLORIANA has removed her scarf and is holding it in her hands)

GLORIANA
(Emphatic in reply)
I'll tell you the man who could protect our internal security----
(An involuntary whipping motion has spread scarf to her side)
Aye, and external security as well.

MOUNTJOY
(Topping her)
You'll accept whatever disappointment and heartache attend the relationship, whatever frustration of your logical hopes for a more appropriate match, and you'll endure this marriage for the sake of your country!

GLORIANA
Meaning?

MOUNTJOY

For compelling reasons, you must marry Tully
Bascom.

GLORIANA
(Gasping with shock)
What? Tully Bascom!

MOUNTJOY
(Pouring out his contrition to GLORIANA)
I realize the terrible blow--his boorish characteristics, manners learned in the National Forest, and
so stubborn!

GLORIANA
(Beginning to recover)
What compelling reasons, Uncle?

MOUNTJOY
When the most popular man in the Duchy is also the
most ambitious, it's a dangerous situation.

GLORIANA
You're confusing me!

MOUNTJOY
You've seen how our people feel about him. They'd
probably do anything he suggested.

GLORIANA
That doesn't mean he's unreasonably ambitious.

MOUNTJOY
(Emphatically)
A young man who--contrary to the intention of his
ruler--wins a war against the United States, is not
to be trusted where ambition is concerned. He's

practically taken personal charge of that terrible
bomb and he won't listen to anyone. You must have
noticed his constant insubordination.
(An awful thought)
Suppose he decided now to form a subversive party?

GLORIANA
Marriage would solve all this?

MOUNTJOY
United to your Grace in matrimony, his popularity
would be directed to the throne. By the same step,
his ambition would automatically be gratified.
(A smile at the thought)
Then perhaps he'd leave matters such as getting
rid of the bomb to trusted ministers.

GLORIANA
(As though he's winning her over)
I confess you're persuasive, Uncle.
(With this, she begins thoughtfully adjusting
the scarf about herself again)

MOUNTJOY
(Warmly approving)
There's a patriot! . . .

GLORIANA
Uncle--it's far from settled.

MOUNTJOY
Oh?

GLORIANA
(Her embarrassment growing)
We don't know how he feels. I mean, he may not
want to marry me.

MOUNTJOY

Of course, he will.

GLORIANA

(More insecure every moment)
He may not like me at all any more.
(Her feminine concern growing)
I know he'd never like me enough to bother with
things that--that show someone cares about you.
(Half indignant)
All he ever talks about now is--duty.

MOUNTJOY

(Unruffled)
That's what we're talking about. In view of the
uncertain times, you should get the matter settled
immediately! This afternoon!

GLORIANA

That's absolutely impossible. His mind is on other
things entirely. There's no way in the world of
getting him to ask.

MOUNTJOY

It's not his place to ask.

GLORIANA

(Puzzled)
Not his place?

MOUNTJOY

As ruler of Grand Fenwick, the proposal must come
from you.

GLORIANA

(Dismayed)
Me?

MOUNTJOY
(Faintly exasperated)
Why can't you regard the matter as completely impersonal?

GLORIANA
(Frankly)
I just don't know, Uncle. . . .

MOUNTJOY
Nonsense. Locate the man at once and tell him he's getting married.

GLORIANA
Must I do it that way, Uncle?

MOUNTJOY
(In a more reasonable tone)
You're our sovereign, Gloriana. I can only urge the custom and example of your ancestors.

GLORIANA
I think I'll go out for a while.

MOUNTJOY
(Keeping his suggestion casual)
It's a lovely day for a walk.

GLORIANA
The way Tully is now, this isn't such an easy walk.
(Starting L)
You'll excuse me----
(She goes off U L)

A MAN CALLED PETER

dramatized by
John McGreevey

from the book by
Catherine Marshall

PETER MARSHALL is a vigorous, youthful man in his late thirties. His smile is infectious and he speaks with a trace of a Scottish burr. He regards his ministry as a deep and enveloping duty.

CATHERINE MARSHALL, his wife, is a pretty woman in her late twenties. Whenever she chides Peter it is done in a spirit of affectionate humor, never sharp or caustic.

The scene is the living room of the Manse, the Marshalls' pastoral residence in Washington, D. C.

PETER is sitting in a chair with an afghan over his knees. Some visitors have just left and, after a moment, CATHERINE speaks.

CATHERINE

Isn't that wonderful?

PETER

The surprising thing to me, Kate, is that so few husbands and wives ask God's help when their marriages are failing.

CATHERINE

(Smoothing afghan over Peter's legs)
They won't take the time to discover what His grace can do.

62

PETER

(Catching her hand)

Of course, first, there must be agreement between them.

CATHERINE

(Not meeting his eyes)

Of course.

PETER

It doesn't do for the wife to beg Him for one thing while all the time the husband's asking for something contrary.

CATHERINE

I know.

PETER

(Urgently)

Kate--are we praying toward the same end?

CATHERINE

We both want you well and strong again.

PETER

True. But short of that----

CATHERINE

(Freeing her hand and moving C)

I don't want anything short of that.

PETER

Kate--a long, long time ago, in Scotland, I made a bargain with God.

CATHERINE

(Facing away from PETER)

Yes. I know.

PETER
I gave my life to God for Him to use wherever, however he wanted.

CATHERINE
Yes. But----

PETER
There were no if's, and's or but's. I put myself completely in God's hands. I promised to give my best to the ministry, leaving the result, including my health, entirely up to God.

CATHERINE
(Facing him, fighting for control)
Peter . . .

PETER
(Insistently)
My best, Kate.

CATHERINE
(In tears)
Your best demands too much of you.
(Moves to his side)
You know what the doctor has said. . . .

PETER
(Quietly)
The doctor isn't concerned in this bargain of mine.

CATHERINE
And what about me? Am I concerned?

PETER
(Reaching out and taking her hand)

Of course you are!
(CATHERINE sinks to her knees beside his
chair)
Oh, Kate! It's so important that we be in agreement on this.

CATHERINE
You can serve him, Peter, but in new ways--ways
that won't strain your heart. If you tried to preach
and work as you did before, it would be throwing
your life away!

PETER
Not if I were serving Him!

CATHERINE
There are many kinds of service.

PETER
You want me to avoid those in trouble? You want
me to refuse to involve myself with men and women
who desperately need me? You want me to be a
narrow, limited man--a minister who always thinks
first of himself? Is that what you want?

CATHERINE
(Pushing to her feet)
I want you to live! That's all I want.
(Moves away from him, toward fireplace, her
face covered)
I just want you to live!
(Leans against mantel, her head bowed)

PETER
(Staring at her with compassion)
Kate . . .
(Catherine's weeping subsides)

I'm sorry. I don't mean to hurt you.

CATHERINE
(Turning and coming back to him)
I know, dearest. I want to feel as you do--but I'm
weak.
(Takes his hand)
Maybe I've asked God for too little. Maybe He
wants to cure your heart, so you won't have to lead
a limited life.

PETER
Perhaps. But, dear, it's for Him to decide.

CATHERINE
(Impulsively raising his hand and kissing it)
Forgive me.
(Moves C, wiping her eyes)
I scold the others for tiring you and then I come in
and stage a scene.

PETER
Stop blaming yourself, Kate. And don't worry.
God will show you the way when the time comes.
He always does.

CATHERINE
I'm too impatient.
(Moves U L)
I'd better check on Peter John. Anything I can do
for you, dear?

PETER
(Grinning)
You might get me a miner's lamp to penetrate this
gloom!

CATHERINE

All right!
    (Moves back to window)
I'll pull the drapes. But you're to stay in that chair.
    (Pulls back drapes, admitting a flood of sun-
    shine. PETER snaps off lamp)
There.

PETER

    (Slyly)
Now--if you'll get my radio and telephone----

CATHERINE

No! Positively not! Relax and content yourself!

PETER

Yes, Simon Legree!
    (Picks up book Nancy brought)
"Silence is Golden."
    (Opens it)
Fools' gold!

RALLY ROUND THE FLAG, BOYS!

a comedy by

David Rogers

adapted from the novel by

Max Shulman

MAGGIE LARKIN is a stunning-looking young lady. She is a teacher at the local school and is Guido's fiancée. Maggie wears attractive clothes and is rather intense on the subject of child psychology.

LIEUTENANT GUIDO DI MAGGIO is young and good-looking and a second lieutenant in the Army. Putnam's Landing is his home town and he is engaged (off and on) to Maggie.

The play occurs in Putnam's Landing, a small town in Connecticut. It is a pleasant evening in spring. The scene is at the Town Hall which has been decorated for a party.

> MAGGIE enters from left and crosses to GUIDO.

MAGGIE

(Shyly)

Hello, Guido . . .

GUIDO

Maggie! Maggie, you came to the welcoming party.

MAGGIE

Well, I wasn't going to--and then I decided to and

not to--and finally to. Honest, I had my dress on and off five times, but finally I decided I better forgive you before my hair was a complete wreck.

GUIDO
(Unable to believe his good luck)
You--you're forgiving me--you--with those beautiful teeth----

MAGGIE
Yes, Guido. Frankly, at that Town Meeting, when you spoke so--well, you weakened me.

GUIDO
I did?

MAGGIE
Yes. You looked so small and sweet standing up there in the middle of all that hostility . . . and then--then suddenly--you converted them--you took that steaming brew of people who hated you . . .

GUIDO
Oh, they hated me!

MAGGIE
And you made them love you. And frankly, that weakened me.

GUIDO
Oh, Maggie, this isn't the time or the place but I want to tell you, I love you. I'll go into it in more detail later.

MAGGIE
And then, finally, you know what did it finally?

GUIDO

No. What?

MAGGIE

Grace Bannerman.

GUIDO

Mrs. Bannerman?

MAGGIE

Yes. Two nights ago I was babysitting with the
Bannerman children and frankly, they upset me.
They were too good, too honest, too sweet. You
know what I mean?

GUIDO

No.

MAGGIE

Well, I mean they were repressing. Children are
normally selfish, grasping, inconsiderate--and her
little boys were so adorable. I had to tell her how
sick they were bound to grow up. When a child re-
presses things, his real feelings always come out
eventually--in asthma or colitis or rheumatism or
something.

GUIDO

You told her that? Their mother?

MAGGIE

Well, it was the most wonderful experience of my
whole life--because--because she told me I was
wrong!

GUIDO

No!

MAGGIE

Yes! Imagine! Mrs. Bannerman taught me more about child psychology than I had learned in my entire life. And she has three children!

GUIDO

When did she have time to learn about child psychology?

MAGGIE

I can't imagine. But, with my new-found knowledge, I went to see Mr. Vandenberg, the principal, and I told him from now on I'm going to be completely sensible and practical and not allow mudpies. And I got my job back!

GUIDO

Maggie, I love you. You just had one fatal flaw and now you've cured it. You're perfect; plumpish and perfect.

MAGGIE

And you forgive me for being such a fool?

GUIDO

Everyone makes mistakes. As long as you've learned your lesson.

MAGGIE

Yes, dear. And we'll never fight again.

GUIDO

(Taking ring from his pocket)
Maggie, will you take the ring back?

MAGGIE

Of course.

(He slips it on her finger. They kiss)

GUIDO
(Breaking kiss)
Sorry, honey, not in front of the troops.

MAGGIE
It's so marvelous that you're stationed here and
we can be together . . . though I'm sure it's going to be a lot of work for you.

GUIDO
Some of it will be fun. Like we're going to sponsor
a Little League team and I'm to manage it.

MAGGIE
(Stiffening)
You're--you're really going to manage a Little
League team?

GUIDO
Of course. What is it, Maggie?

MAGGIE
(Making a determined effort)
It's nothing--nothing. Tell me your other plans.

GUIDO
(Wondering what's the matter with her)
Well, I thought I'd take the Boy Scouts on a camp-
ing trip . . .

MAGGIE
That's lovely. . . .
(Tightly)
A Little League team with games and a world series
and champions and everything?

GUIDO
(Confused)
Well--sure--that's what Little League is. . . .

MAGGIE
(Containing herself)
I see.
(Stiffens and clamps her lips tightly)

GUIDO
Then I thought I'd take any of the high school kids
who are interested in electronics on a tour of the
base. Show them how everything works.

MAGGIE
(Bursting out)
Guido! No!

GUIDO
Why not? I won't show them anything classified.

MAGGIE
Not the electronics! The Little League!

GUIDO
That's just baseball. It's outdoors. It's healthy.

MAGGIE
Healthy! I can't--I've tried not to say it, but I
can't! Don't you know Little League is the greatest
single menace to the mental health of America's
children? I will not let you be a party to it.

GUIDO
Oh, no! Not again! Not so soon!

MAGGIE
All that emphasis on winning. All that tension. All

that pressure! Never mind playing the game. Just win! Be champions! Let the little nerves crack, the innocent hearts break, but win!

GUIDO
(Losing patience)
Maggie, I love you! But I can't be engaged to a nut!

MAGGIE
(Taking off ring)
And the bleachers full of parents acting out their thwarted aggressions, screaming at their children. Fight! Fight! Win! Win! Never mind the trauma --never mind the . . .
>   (She hands him the ring, pulls a ragged
>   piece of tissue out of her purse, puts it to
>   her eyes and runs off into the crowd)

PORTRAIT OF JENNIE

by

Bettye Knapp

from the book by

Robert Nathan

JENNIE is the central figure in the hauntingly beautiful story about a girl who didn't age in the normal way, and the painter, EBEN, to whom art involved showing the unseen beauties of the world we live in. The gradual and delicate growth and change in the extraordinary love between the girl and the painter increases as the play moves from a hard bench in Central Park in the winter of 1932 to the artist's simple studio. The play has enormous delicacy, charm and nostalgia. In this final scene of the second act, JENNIE has matured to a radiant twenty-one.

(JENNIE knocks on Eben's door)

            EBEN
        (Without turning)
Come in.

            JENNIE
        (Moving to him)
Hello, Eben----

            EBEN
Jennie! Jennie, I've missed you.
        (He takes her hands)

JENNIE

I know. I've missed you, too. It's been longer for me.
(Looks around the room)
At night I've lain awake thinking of this small room. I used to have the most dreadful dream--that I was walking and walking and couldn't find you. And right now as I came down the sidewalk I had the most awful feeling that perhaps you weren't here-- and that perhaps you didn't want to see me again.

EBEN

How could you ever think that?

JENNIE

You do want to see me again, don't you, Eben?

EBEN

Jennie--Mr. Mathews just took the portrait of you. I couldn't let it go before today. I had to have some part of you here----

JENNIE

Then you've sold it! Oh, that's wonderful. Aren't you happy?

EBEN

I'm happy because you're here.

JENNIE

Let's do something special, shall we? To celebrate your success? I haven't long to stay with you. You see, I'm being sent abroad--to a finishing school-- for two years.

EBEN

Two years?

JENNIE

I don't want to go, but I have to.

EBEN

And then?

JENNIE

I'm going to hurry and then some day I'll be as old
as you are.

EBEN

I'm twenty-eight.

JENNIE

I know it.   And so will I be--then.

EBEN

You've changed so much in these three months.
You're beautiful, Jennie, and poised and self-
assured, and there isn't any more fear----

JENNIE

That's because of you, Eben.
            (She twirls)
Let's go on a picnic.   Somewhere in the country.
It's something we've never done before.

EBEN

As though we've done very much of anything before,
Jennie.

JENNIE

There will be flowers and a stream----

EBEN

I can get Gus to take us in his cab, and Mr. Moore,
at the restaurant, will make us a lunch.

(JENNIE walks around the room, a quiet
smile on her lips)
What are you thinking?

JENNIE
(Turns to him)
I'm thinking how beautiful the world is. And how
it keeps being beautiful--no matter what happens
to us. It was never made for anything but beauty,
Eben, whether we lived now or long ago. The spring
comes year after year, for us or for Egypt. The
sun goes down in the same green, lovely sky; the
birds sing--for us or yesterday--or for tomorrow.

EBEN
Tomorrow. But when is tomorrow, Jennie?

JENNIE
Does it matter? It's always. This was tomorrow
once. Oh, Eben, promise me you'll never forget?

EBEN
Where I come from
Nobody knows;
And where I'm going
Everything goes.

JENNIE
The wind blows,
The sea flows--
And God knows.

I think He knows, don't you, Eben?
(She lifts her lips and kisses him gently)
That's to remember today.

EBEN
As though it could ever be forgotten.

JENNIE

I sail on the "Mauretania" in the morning.

EBEN

So soon?

JENNIE

Tell me about Paris. You were there, weren't
you? My school is in Passy--is that near where
you were? Tell me what to see and what to do--
so that some day we'll have done it all together----

EBEN

(Takes her hand, and they sit on the cot)
I had a wonderful room near the Seine. It was a
room like the prow of a ship. Perhaps I can show
it to you some time. And perhaps I'll take you to
the Luxembourg and the Fair at Neuilly--and we'll
dance together in the Place Pigalle on Bastille Day
and drink new wine in the spring----

JENNIE

It's going to be such fun----

EBEN

Most of the time I was pretty broke, and so was
Arne. But it didn't really matter. Being poor
wasn't at all difficult. One accepted it the way one
accepted the morning light.

JENNIE

I used to tell the girls at school about you. That
you were very handsome----

EBEN

(Rises)
Don't be silly.

JENNIE

(Rises)

And that you're a great artist and that you nearly starved to death. They loved that part. They thought it was very romantic.

EBEN

Amazing how anyone with a full stomach can look upon hunger as being romantic.

JENNIE

Did you like Paris as well as the Cape?

EBEN

The Cape is really my home. It has a special smell and sound. Like the storms that sing across the dunes and the thunder of the surf right below Arne's shanty.

JENNIE

I saw a picture of the Cape once and all of a sudden I felt it was a sad place. It made me cry.

EBEN

But it isn't a sad place, Jennie. It's a place where children play and dig for clams and lovers walk along the beach at low tide and sea gulls swoop down and talk to the waves.

JENNIE

And where there are frightful storms! I wouldn't like it, Eben. I shall never go there. Unless----

EBEN

Unless?

JENNIE

Let's not talk about it. I didn't want to remember it.

EBEN

Unless what, Jennie?

JENNIE

Unless I thought you really needed me.

EBEN

How would you know that, Jennie?

JENNIE

I shan't write to you, Eben. But the time will go quickly. It always does. Soon it will all be a to-morrow.

EBEN

I'll wait for you, Jennie.

JENNIE

I know----

EBEN

I have the feeling that the world and you and I are one. That there is so much unsaid, and yet so little that needs saying........

JENNIE

Wherever I am in the world, we'll be together.
          (He puts his arms around her and they kiss
          gently)
But we have the whole rest of the day, Eben! I'm going to make a daisy chain and cover you with lady-bugs and race you over meadows and wade in the stream!

EBEN

Jennie, it sounds wonderful!
          (He kisses her again)

THE DIRECTOR SPEAKS

on

LISTENING

Fortunate were the actors who lived before the age of the amplifier, fortunate at least in performing for audiences that were good listeners. Our technological paradise of computers, motors and jets is, I think, the noisiest environment which man has ever created for himself. And Nature, in her kindly compensating fashion, has shielded man from the din about him by dulling his ability to listen.

Man, in turn, though not as wise but almost as quick, has solved this problem of getting through to the callous-eared public by revving up the amplifiers on everything from a pop singer's microphone to the radio and television commercials.

Could anything in sensory response be worse for the living theatre, whose modus operandi, we should always remember, is based on the premise that the words of the play will be projected by the actor into the consciousness, and it is hoped the emotions, of the audience.

Now don't suggest to me that we can join the no-talent singer and the non-projecting public speaker and solve our problem with microphones. The amplifier must not be allowed near a play and its actors. I have never seen it done without bringing ruin to the true concept of living theatre.

What we can do is to be very concerned with listening--both our own and our audience's. The one can help the other. For the actor it is the larger assignment, for he must listen in three ways.

First, he listens as a technician to hear im-

mediately and accurately the words spoken or implied by his fellow players. This is an inner, constant process invisible to the spectator but essential to a clear, soundly-based performance.

Next the actor listens in character. In your
study with these scenes you will soon see that
Helena's listening in "Look Back in Anger" is as
different from Bernadette's as the two characters
differ one from the other. The High Lama's way
of listening in "Lost Horizon" is an almost totally
different process from that of Gloriana in "The
Mouse That Roared." Working and building this
individuality in listening pays, of course, a fine
dividend to the intricate process of characterization.

Finally, the player listens to build scenes and
to better audience listening by good example. You
need look no further for the antithesis of this than
to attend a performance by a tired road company.
All the words are there, the business is complete,
but if the actors no longer listen--then the play is
in danger. It begins to look and sound like actors
acting--which can be a very poor aesthetic experience.

But when the actor listens in all three ways,
constantly, effectively and sincerely, two splendid things tend to happen. The character and the
scene move toward fulfillment--and the audience,
following as audiences are wont to follow, listens
more effectively and their involvement in the play
increases.

LUTHER

by

John Osborne

In this powerful play, the struggle between Martin Luther and the forces of Christendom mounts from crescendo to crescendo. In Act Two, Scene Four, the confrontation is between LUTHER and CAJETAN. Cajetan, whose real name is Thomas De Vio, is head of the Dominican Order and the Pope's highest representative in Germany. He is questioning Luther about his sermons and writings and is surprised to find Luther so young. Cajetan is amazed that the University should have conferred a doctorate on anyone so inexperienced as Martin Luther must have been.

The play, which won the Drama Critics Award, covers a period of twenty-one years. In this scene, which occurs at Augsburg, Luther is thirty-five. He is a man of great inner strength which seems to come from his dedication to his convictions.

Cajetan admonishes Luther for having such a lack of trust in his mother church that he had felt it necessary to ask the Emperor for safe conduct. However, he proceeds in a civilized and conciliatory tone.

CAJETAN

Oh, my dear, dear son, this is such a ridiculous, unnecessary business for us all to be mixed up in. It's such a tedious, upsetting affair, and what purpose is there in it? Your entire order in Germany has been brought into disgrace. I have my job to

do, and, make no mistake, it isn't all honey for an
Italian legate in your country. You know how it is,
people are inclined to resent you. Nationalist feeling and all that--which I respect--but it does com-
plicate one's task to the point where this kind of
issue thrown in for good measure simply makes
the whole operation impossible. You know what I
mean? I mean, there's your Duke Frederick, an
absolutely fair, honest man, if ever there was one,
and one his holiness values and esteems particularly. Well, his holiness instructed me to present the
Duke with the Golden Rose of Virtue, so you can
see. As well as even more indulgences for his
Castle Church. But what happens now? Because
of all this unpleasantness and the uproar it's caused
throughout Germany, the Duke's put in an extreme-
ly difficult position about accepting it. Naturally,
he wants to do the right thing by everyone. But
he's not going to betray you or anything like that,
however much he's set his heart on that Golden Rose,
all these years. And, of course, he's perfectly
right. I know he has the greatest regard for you
and for some of your ideas--even though, as he's
told me--he doesn't agree with a lot of them. No,
I can only respect him for all that. So, you see,
my dear son, what a mess we are in. Now, what
are we going to do? Um? The Duke is unhappy.
I am unhappy, his holiness is unhappy, and you,
my son, you are unhappy.

MARTIN
(Formal, as if it were a prepared speech)
Most worthy father, in obedience to the summons
of his papal holiness, and in obedience to the orders of my gracious lord, the Elector of Saxony,
I have come before you as a submissive and dutiful
son of the holy Catholic church, and if I have been

wrong, to submit to your instruction in the truth.

CAJETAN
(Impatiently)
My son, you have upset all Germany with your dispute about indulgences. I know you're a very learned doctor of the Holy Scriptures, and that you've already aroused a few supporters. But if you wish to remain a member of the Church, and to find a gracious father in the Pope, you'd better listen. I have here, in front of me, three propositions which, by the command of our holy father, Pope Leo the Tenth, I shall put to you now. First, you must admit your faults, and retract all your errors and sermons. Secondly, you must promise to abstain from propagating your opinions at any time in the future. And, thirdly, you must behave generally with greater moderation, and avoid anything which might cause offense or grieve and disturb the Church.

MARTIN
May I be allowed to see the Pope's instruction?

CAJETAN
No, my dear son, you many not. All you are required to do is confess your errors, keep a strict watch on your words, and not go back like a dog to his vomit. Then, once you have done that, I have been authorized by our most holy father to put everything to rights again.

MARTIN
I understand all that. But I'm asking you to tell me where I have erred.

CAJETAN
If you insist.
(Rattling off, very fast)

Just to begin with, here are two propositions you have advanced, and which you will have to retract before anything else. First, "the treasure of indulgences does not consist of the sufferings and torments of our Lord Jesus Christ." Second, "The man who receives the holy sacrament must have faith in the grace that is presented to him." Enough?

MARTIN

I rest my case entirely on Holy Scriptures.

CAJETAN

The Pope alone has power and authority over all those things.

MARTIN

Except Scripture.

CAJETAN

Including Scripture. What do you mean?........

MARTIN

But I am a man, and I may be deceived, so I am willing to receive instruction where I have been mistaken.

CAJETAN

(Angrily)

Save your arrogance, my son, there'll be a better place to use it. I can have you sent to Rome, and let any of your German princes try to stop me! He'll find himself standing outside the gates of Heaven like a leper........I'm not here to enter into a disputation with you, now or at any other time. The Roman Church is the apex of the world, Spiritual and temporal, and it may constrain with its secular arm any of those who have once received the faith and gone astray. Surely, I don't have to remind you that it is not bound to use reason to fight and destroy rebels.

(He sighs)

My son, it's getting late. You must retract. Believe me, I simply want to see this business ended as quickly as possible.

MARTIN

Some interests are furthered by finding truth, others by destroying it. I don't care--what pleases or displeases the Pope. He is a man........

CAJETAN

All right, Martin, I will argue with you if you want me to--or rather, I'll put something to you, because there is something more than your safety or your life involved, something bigger than you and me talking together in this room at this time. Oh, it's fine for someone like you to criticize and start tearing down Christendom, but tell me this, what will you build in its place?

MARTIN

An infected place is best scoured out, and so you pray for healthy tissue and something sturdy and clean for what was crumbling and full of filth.

CAJETAN

My dear son, don't you see? You would destroy the perfect unity of the world........Suppose you did destroy the Pope. What do you think would become of you?

MARTIN

I don't know.

CAJETAN

Exactly, you wouldn't know what to do because you

need him, Martin, you need to hunt him more than
he needs his silly wild boar. Well? There have
always been popes, and there always will be even
if they're called something else. They'll have them
for people like you. You're not a good old revolu-
tionary, my son, you're just a common rebel, a
very different animal. You fight the Pope, not because he's too big, but because for your needs he's
not big enough.........Why, some poor, deluded
creature might even come to you as a leader of their
revolution, but you don't want to break rules, you
want to make them. I've read some of your sermons on faith. Do you know all they say to me?

                    MARTIN
No.

                    CAJETAN
They say: I am a man struggling for certainty,
struggling insanely like a man in a fit, an animal
trapped to the bone with doubt.
            (MARTIN seems about to have a physical
            struggle with himself)

                    MARTIN
Your eminence, forgive me. I'm tired after my
journey--I think I might faint soon----

                    CAJETAN
Don't you see what could happen out of all this?
Men could be cast out and left to themselves forever, helpless and frightened! That's what would
become of them without their Mother Church--with
all its imperfections, Peter's rock. Without it
they'd be helpless and unprotected. Allow them
their sins, my son, their petty indulgences, they're
unimportant to the comfort we receive----

MARTIN
(Somewhat hysterical)
Comfort! It--doesn't concern me!

CAJETAN
We live in thick darkness, and it grows thicker.
How will men find God if they are left to themselves,
each man abandoned and only known to himself?

MARTIN
They'll have to try........
       (He prostrates himself, and then kneels
       up. CAJETAN is distressed but in control)

CAJETAN
You know, Martin, a time will come when a man
will no longer be able to say "I speak Latin and am
a Christian" and go his way in peace. There will
come frontiers, barriers of all kinds--between men
--and there'll be no end to them.
    (MARTIN rises and goes out)

EPITAPH FOR GEORGE DILLON

by

John Osborne and Anthony Creighton

It is autumn in the Elliot family home near London. The time is the present.

BARNEY EVANS is nearly fifty, and has never had a doubt about anything in all that time. He wears a rather old Crombie overcoat, expensive but crumpled suit, thick horn-rimmed glasses, and a rakish Homburg hat.

GEORGE DILLON is a little over thirty, boyish, yet every year his age. He is not good-looking but has an anti-romantic kind of charm. He wears everyday clothes.

> BARNEY EVANS comes in through the front door and speaks.

BARNEY
Anyone there? Anyone at home? I say?

GEORGE
In here. Come in here.

BARNEY
Where?
> (To sitting room door)

In here? Oh, yes. Good. Sorry to butt in on you like this. The fact is----
> (GEORGE rises)

Oh, yes, you must be who I am looking for.

GEORGE
Oh? Sit down, will you?

BARNEY

No, no, no--I can't stop a minute. I found I was
passing your door, so I thought I'd just pop in for
a few words. . . . I'm just on my way to Brighton,
as a matter of fact.

GEORGE

For the weekend?

BARNEY

Business and pleasure.
        (Thoughtfully)
Business--mostly. Look, I'll come straight to the
point, Mr.----

GEORGE

Dillon. George Dillon.

BARNEY

        (Producing a script from his pocket)
Oh, yes. It's on here. George Dillon. Been in
the business long?

GEORGE

Well--a few----

BARNEY

Thought so. Didn't ever play the Palace, Westport,
did you?

GEORGE

No, I didn't.

BARNEY

Face seemed familiar. Well, now--to get down to
it----

GEORGE

Is that my script you've got there?

BARNEY

That's right.

GEORGE

How on earth did you get hold of it?

BARNEY

Andy gave it to me.

GEORGE

Andy?

BARNEY

Andre Tatlock. You know him, don't you?

GEORGE

Oh--the Trident. Is he a friend of yours then?

BARNEY

Andy? I knew him when he was a chorus boy at the
old Tivoli. You wouldn't remember that. Why, it
was me put him back on his feet after that bit of
trouble. You know that, don't you?

GEORGE

Yes.

BARNEY

He hadn't even got a set of underwear--I had to get
that for him. Silly fellow!
        (Sucks his breath deprecatingly)
Still, he's all right now. That was my idea--that
bar, you know. Oh, he did it up himself, mind you
--Andy's very clever with his hands. But it was

my idea. And now that bar's packed every night. Can't get within a mile of the place. He doesn't have to worry whether he puts on a show or not. . . . And as long as he can find enough authors willing to back their own plays with hard cash, he won't go without his bottle of gin, believe me.

(Produces a packet of cheroots)

Got a match? I take it you don't have any capital of your own?

GEORGE

Right.

BARNEY

Yes, he said you'd told him you hadn't any money to put up yourself.

GEORGE

(Lighting his cheroot for him)

I rang him about it weeks ago. I remember he said he liked the play.

BARNEY

Liked it? That's a good one. Andy doesn't read plays--he just puts 'em on. Provided of course he can make something out of it. Now, I've read this play of yours, and I'm interested. Are you willing to listen to a proposition?

GEORGE

Of course.

BARNEY

By the way, I'm Barney Evans. You've heard of me, of course.

(GEORGE hesitates, but BARNEY doesn't wait)

Now, Andy's a friend of mine. I've done a lot for him--but he's only in the business in a very small way. Oh, he does himself all right. But it's small stuff. You wouldn't get anywhere much with him-- you know that, of course?

GEORGE
Yes.

BARNEY
I'm only interested in the big money. Small stuff's not worth my while. I take it you are interested in money?

GEORGE
Is that a rhetorical question?

BARNEY
Eh?

GEORGE
Yes, I am.

BARNEY
That's all right then. I don't want to waste my time. This is the first play you've written?

GEORGE
My seventh----

BARNEY
Dialogue's not bad, but these great long speeches-- that's a mistake. People want action, excitement. I know--you think you're Bernard Shaw. But where's he today? Eh? People won't listen to him. Any- way, politics are out--you ought to know that. Now, take "My Skin Is My Enemy!" I've got that on the

road at the moment. That and "Slasher Girl!"

GEORGE

"My Skin Is My . . . " Oh, yes, it's about the color bar problem, isn't it?

BARNEY

Well, yes--but you see it's first-class entertainment! Played to six hundred pounds at Llandinrod Wells last week. Got the returns in my pocket now. It's controversial, I grant you, but it's the kind of thing people pay money to see. That's the kind of thing you want to write.

GEORGE

Still, I imagine you've got to be just a bit liberal-minded to back a play like that........

BARNEY

I know young fellows like you. You're interested in ideals still. Idealists. Don't think I don't know. I was an idealist myself once. . . . But, make no mistake--ideals didn't get me where I am.

GEORGE

No?

BARNEY

You spend your time dabbling in politics, and vote in some ragged-arsed bunch of nobodies who can't hardly pronounce the queen's English properly, and where are you? Where are you? Nowhere. Crushed down in the mob, indistinguishable from the masses. What's the good of that to a young man with talent?

GEORGE

I should have thought you had a vested interest in

the masses.

BARNEY

Most certainly. I admit it. And that's why I believe in education. Education--it always shows,
and it always counts. . . .

> (He sprays his ash over the floor thought-
> fully)

To get back to this play of yours. I think it's got
possibilities, but it needs rewriting. Acts One and
Two won't be so bad, provided you cut out all the
highbrow stuff, give it pace--you know: dirty it up
a bit, you see.

GEORGE

I see.

BARNEY

Third act's construction is weak. I could help you
there--and I'd do it for quite a small consideration
because I think you've got something. You know
that's a very good idea--getting the girl in the family
way.

GEORGE

You think so?

BARNEY

Never fails. Get someone in the family way in the
Third Act--you're halfway there. I suppose you
saw "I Was a Drug Fiend"?

GEORGE

No.

BARNEY

Didn't you, really? No wonder you write like you

do! I thought everyone had seen that! That was
my show, too. Why, we were playing to three and
four thousand a week on the twice nightly circuit
with that. That's the sort of money you want to
play to. Same thing in that: Third Act--girl's in
the family way. Course, in that play, her elder
sister goes out as a missionary, and ends up dying
upside down on an ant hill in her birthday suit. I
spent six months in the South of France on what I
made out of that show.

    (Motor horn toots outside)
Here, I'll have to be going. As I say, you rewrite
it as I tell you; maybe we can do business together
and make some money for both of us. I'll read it
through again, and drop you a line. In the mean-
time, I should redraft the whole thing, bearing in
mind what I said. Right?

GEORGE
I'll have to think about it. The fact is--I'm not
feeling up to much at the moment. I'm completely
broke, for one thing.

BARNEY
O. K. then. You'll be hearing from me. You take
my advice--string along with me. I know this business inside and out. You forget about starving for
art's sake. That won't keep you alive five minutes.
You've got to be ruthless.

    (Moves into hall)
Yes, there's no other word for it--absolutely ruthless.

    (GEORGE follows him. BARNEY picks up
    his hat from stand and knocks over vase.
    He looks down at the pieces absentminded-
    ly)
Oh, sorry. Now you take Hitler--the greatest man

that ever lived! Don't care what anyone says--you can't get away from it. He had the right idea, you've got to be ruthless, and it's the same in this business. Course he may have gone a bit too far sometimes.

GEORGE
Think so?

BARNEY
I do. I do think so, most definitely. Yes, he over-reached himself, no getting away from it. That's where all great men make their mistake--they over-reach themselves.
>   (Car horn toots insistently)

Hullo, blimey, she'll start smashing the windows in a minute.
>   (GEORGE follows him as he hurries to
>   door)

Well, you just remember what I said. Tell you what --I'll give you a ring on Monday. I'll be busy all the weekend.
>   (Opens door)

By the way, that girl?

GEORGE
What girl?

BARNEY
The girl in your play--what do you call her?

GEORGE
Oh, you mean----

BARNEY
Build her up. Build her right up. She's--she's a prostitute really, isn't she?

GEORGE

Well----

BARNEY

Of course she is! I've just had an idea--a new slant.
Your title, what is it?

(He doesn't wait for a reply)

Anyway, it won't bring anybody in. I've just thought
of a smashing title. You know what we'll call it?
"Telephone Tart." That's it! "Telephone Tart."
You string along with me, George, I'll see you're
all right.

(Exit)

THE GREAT BIG DOORSTEP

by

Frances Goodrich and Albert Hackett

The COMMODORE is a Cajun, one of that happy, charming breed found in south Louisiana. His responsibilities as head of the Crochet family fall lightly upon him. The contrast between his well-fed look and the rest of his family testifies to this.

DEWEY CROCHET is The Commodore's brother and has fared better economically, especially during the time when he was a Mississippi River pilot. He is a large man and well dressed--this being in sharp contrast with The Commodore. His speech has little of the rich Cajun qualities we hear in The Commodore.

The scene takes place outside the Crochet shack in Grass Margin, Louisiana.

COMMODORE
(Crossing to him)

Drink up, Dewey. And you know what? After we eat, I'm gunna take you up and show you that new house. I'm gunna show you the room we keep jiss for you.

DEWEY
(Belligerently)

What kinda house is that, that you can get for sixty dollar!

COMMODORE
(Sitting beside DEWEY)

101

That's jiss the back taxes. It's a lovely place. You wait till you see it. Of course, Shoepick ain' lifted a finger to care for it. He would have left it long ago, excepp his papa is buried in the front yard.

DEWEY
What is it? A cemetery?

COMMODORE
Hush up. I didn't say people buried there.

DEWEY
You tell me his papa buried there!

COMMODORE
Yes. His papa. His papa! Jiss one man!

DEWEY
(Nothing but an argument will satisfy him now) I don' like it.

COMMODORE
Shoepick's papa was a fine man. We glad he's buried there, under the trees that he plant. That's where he want to be, and that's where he gunna stay. Lissen, will you? What I want you to know, there'll be plenny of room there for you.
(The COMMODORE drinks. DEWEY gives him a look. The COMMODORE looks at DEWEY, embarrassed as he realizes how it must have sounded)

DEWEY
Better be careful of that wine. It might have ants in it.

COMMODORE
Oh, hush up the ants! Everybody got ants. The

rich like the poor. The Protesan like the Catlick.
I never see an ant take the road when he see a pilot
comin'.

DEWEY
Well, lemme tell you, they ain' no ants on me. I
ain' sittin' 'round loafin' so they get on. I work too
hard.

COMMODORE
(Provoked)
Some talks about hard work, never did nothin' strin-
gent in all their born days' life.

DEWEY
You don' get to be a pilot unless you work.

COMMODORE
(Heatedly, rising)
Lissen! I was a pilot. I know all about it. Don'
try to put that over on me! You don' know what
hard work is!

DEWEY
Is that so! So that's what you think of me!
(He gets up, staggers over below the table, goes
up to the steps, picks up his shoes and tie, etc.,
from below the steps)
Okay! Okay!

COMMODORE
What do pilots do excepp eat and sleep and hardly
ever lay a hand on the wheel?
(The battle is on. DEWEY goes to the upper
right end of the table)

DEWEY
Is that so? I'd like to see you swing a big tanker

in the head wind with an empty bow like I hadda do
the other day.

COMMODORE
(Moving R, to the upper left end of the table)
Me, I could tell you things about that river. I know
every inch of it. When I went up that river----

DEWEY
(Interrupting, hitting below the belt)
When you went up that river you was asleep. They
couldn't truss you, they said. You lose a whole
load of mules. 'Cause you was sleepin'. Some of
them ain' been found yet.
(He picks up the funny papers from the ground)

COMMODORE
What! I could still be a pilot if I want to. But I
don' wanna. I rather work for my livin'.

DEWEY
Okay. I'll be shovin' off.
(He goes to the gate)
I'll see you when you want somethin' from me again.
I'm goin' down the road. I'll take these things
where they'll be welcome. I'm afraid to leave them
here. They might draw ants.
(He comes down right of the COMMODORE,
reaching his hand for the Commodore's hat)
That hat! I'll take that hat!

COMMODORE
(Taking off the hat, looking at it, terribly hurt)
Go on! Take it. I don' want your charity!
(He hands it to DEWEY)

DEWEY
(Very dignified)

Lissen, I'd like that skull I gave Arthur.

COMMODORE
(The final blow has landed)
Arthur's skull!
 (The COMMODORE crosses to the downstage
 window. DEWEY follows and stops in front of
 the table)
It's jiss a pity you never brung that pilot husband
for Topal, so you can take him back, too. Here--
 (He goes to DEWEY)
--take your old skull. We took it with a good heart.
It was a token of you, Dewey.
 (DEWEY starts for the gate, but stops when
 the COMMODORE speaks. The COMMODORE
 reaches in his pocket and pulls out the check)
And take this check. I don' want you to lenn us no
money.

DEWEY
 (U L)
No. You can keep that. I already wrote it off for
a loss.

COMMODORE
 (R C)
For a loss! Look, that's how much it is a loss!
 (The COMMODORE tears it into bits and throws
 it to the ground. He looks at it a moment, and
 then turns upstage. DEWEY watches in amaze-
 ment)
Me, I'll never forget this night. Things is never
gunna be the same. Mark my words, Messyou
Dewey Crochet!

A SOUND OF HUNTING

by

Harry Brown

CAPTAIN JOHN TRELAWNY is slim and sober; a perpetual frown is on his face, so that even when he smiles, there are wrinkles in his forehead.

SERGEANT THOMAS CARTER is a good soldier and, like Captain Trelawny, terribly concerned for his men.

It is January, 1944. The scene is the living room of a war-ruined house on the outskirts of Cassino. The Italian campaign is at a climax and its effect is evident on both soldiers.

TRELAWNY

What kind of orders do you understand, anyway?

CARTER

All kinds.

TRELAWNY

Mr. Finley informs me you've taken matters into your own hands. Where's Sergeant Mooney?

CARTER

I thought you knew, Captain. He went out after that gun........

TRELAWNY

All right, Tom, why did they do it?

CARTER

Don't you know?

106

TRELAWNY

No, I don't. I can't understand Mooney. He leaves me no choice. I'll have to prefer charges against him.

CARTER

That won't do any good.

TRELAWNY

It's the only thing I can do. That fool Finley will spread the story all over the Army as soon as he goes back. He'll make it appear that I have no control over my men.

CARTER

Is that what you're worried about?

TRELAWNY

No, Tom, that's not what I'm worried about. I'm just trying to keep this company alive. Why do you think I gave that order? I don't want anything to happen to Small--but I don't want to lose three or four men on a wild-goose chase.

CARTER

You won't.

TRELAWNY

If I don't, it's the damnedest piece of luck in the world. Mooney should know better than to take a chance like that.

CARTER

Mooney does know better.

TRELAWNY

Why didn't you do something? You could have

stopped them.

CARTER

No, I couldn't. Even if I could, I wouldn't.

TRELAWNY

What is this--you wouldn't? Why wouldn't you?

CARTER

I know how they feel, Johnnie. I feel the same way.
You don't know all of it. You haven't been sitting
around here today, watching them grow more nerv-
ous every minute. You should have seen Coke.

TRELAWNY

Coke!

CARTER

Yes. He would have gone out there alone. So
would Mooney--so would any of them.

TRELAWNY

How can I keep a company together when half the
men in it want to commit suicide?

CARTER

None of them wants to commit suicide. They
wouldn't have gone out there if they didn't feel they
had to. We don't like it out there that much.

TRELAWNY

That's not the point. The point is, why wouldn't
you stop them? What's got into you, anyway?

CARTER

I don't know. Maybe it's a kind of love. You see,
Johnnie, you think in terms of a company--I think

in terms of eight men. I live with them. I may very well die with them. I'm closer to them than I ever was to anyone in my family. I know what drove Mooney to go out there. He feels exactly the way I do. He stood it as long as he could and then he just had to go.

TRELAWNY

And took the chance of getting three more men killed.

CARTER

If you want to look at it that way--yes.

TRELAWNY

Tom, I'm responsible for a lot of men--too many men. Every day I have to send them out, and every day I know there'll be those who won't come back. They send fresh-faced kids up here, and I turn them into old men in a week. I see them lying dead in the mud. Every missing face keeps me awake at night. Every death in this company is a knife in my heart. Can you blame me for not wanting Mooney to go out there? Can you blame me for wanting to save three lives?

CARTER

No, I don't blame you. I know how you feel.

TRELAWNY

Then why in hell didn't you stop them?

CARTER

Because if I'd have been here I would have gone with them. Johnnie, this squad is an entity. It isn't Small out there--it's part of that entity. If they don't bring him in or find out what happened

to him they'll never be the same. Don't you see
what I'm driving at? If they leave him out there
it'll be as though they left part of themselves.
There'll be a blank somewhere. They'll feel guilty.
It'll keep them awake the rest of their lives. But
if they bring him in, it'll be all right. Even if they
find him dead, it'll be all right. It'll hurt them--
and they won't forget it--but they'll know they did
all they could. The luck ran out, that's all.

TRELAWNY

It always does.

CARTER

Sure, it always does. It took a little longer this
time. That's the only difference. That's what
makes it harder.

TRELAWNY

I know all that, Tom. What do you want me to do?

CARTER

Leave them alone.

TRELAWNY

Leave them alone--yes, I'll leave them alone. I
don't know what's the matter with me, Tom. I'm
tired. I've had too much of it. I need a long sleep.

CARTER

We all do. We'll get it one of these days.

TRELAWNY

(Suddenly)

That goddamned Finley got under my skin. Why do
they have to bother us up here?

CARTER

I don't know.   It'll work out, won't it?

TRELAWNY

Sure, sure--it'll work out. I guess they'll get back all right, eh?

CARTER

They'll get back.   But I don't think they'll feel too good.

TRELAWNY

Why not?

CARTER

Because I don't think Small made it.

TRELAWNY

(Bitterly)

God damn it to hell.

THE DIRECTOR SPEAKS

on

CONCENTRATION

If I chose the one human attribute which seems most often to determine the difference between mediocrity and excellence, omitting from the consideration talent and chance, I think I would select the ability to concentrate.

It has an important bearing on many activities and pursuits and we of theatre must consider it carefully and well. While the latent ability to concentrate may have a general median or norm, its degree of development is far from uniform. We know that in formal study teachers often find an answer to rate of achievement in "He or she does does not concentrate."

We need no further example than the game of golf, which asks physically of players not much more than the strength to lift a stick, hit a ball and repeat the process until the white ball is in the black cup. You may say that some golf champions are big, strong men and I can show you champions who are small, weak men--but I think I can promise you that in all the champions there is a highly developed ability to concentrate. The duffer who cannot even keep his head down would do well to consciously develop his power of concentration.

For this is a willed process: we do not happen to concentrate--we have to make ourselves do it.

There is a double return in the practice of concentration: it makes for good work, and, using and exploring the full powers of an individual, tends to raise these powers to higher levels of performance.

It is possible for many to live long lives and never consciously work at concentration. And yet to all come moments of highly efficient concentration when high emotional stress, such as anger, grief, danger, focuses the human mechanism into single, efficient points of attention.

Thus your work as an actor is closely related to your ability to concentrate. As you improve it, there should be a rise in the general quality of your work. And since there is a geometrical ratio between the intensity of emotion and the completeness of concentration, the very content of the craft can assist in mastery.

As you work on these scenes you will find deepening concentration paying fine rewards. It will speed your memorization, thus bringing you sooner to the real satisfactions of acting.

The depth of concentration is rarely more obvious than in rehearsal of a scene. Early in the timetable the slightest error--a twisted line, a misused name--will at once throw the actors out of the play, often with an amused reaction, revealing the shallowness of concentration.

With work, study and rehearsal this physical and mental driving force can become so strong that in performance the laughter and applause of the audience, the rustle of programs, a slow light or sound effect--even a bad cue--cannot stop the well-prepared actor from the "swift completion of his appointed rounds," as our friends in the Post Office used to say.

TIGHT LITTLE ISLAND

by

Sherman L. Sergel

Founded on the book by

Sir Compton MacKenzie

PEGGY MACROON is a bright attractive girl in her twenties. She is the Postmaster's daughter.

CATRIONA MACLEOD, Peggy's friend, is two years younger. The girls are caught up in the gay adventures of this diverting and uninhibited comedy. Because of the War, the Big and Little Todday Islands, part of the Hebrides, have been without a drop of whisky to drink. Then a ship filled with Scotch whisky comes to rest on a nearby rock and the islanders get busy.

In this scene the girls are waiting for the men to return from salvaging the precious cargo. They are in the Post Office home of Joseph Macroon, Peggy's father.

>   PEGGY is looking out the window. CATRI-
>   ONA is furious. She is pacing the floor
>   and smoking one cigarette after another.

CATRIONA

Any sign?

PEGGY

I can't really see yet--the fog. Perhaps they haven't

114

had enough time.

CATRIONA
Yes, time.
> (She puts her cigarette out)

I wonder if George went.

PEGGY
He may have.

CATRIONA
I doubt it.

PEGGY
He could be there.

CATRIONA
He's probably home, tending the hens.

PEGGY
> (Leaving the window and putting an arm
> around CATRIONA)

Now, Catriona.

CATRIONA
Oh, Peggy, you know he's home and so do I.

PEGGY
He may be helping.

CATRIONA
Possibly, but not likely.
> (She drops into the easy chair)

I wish I didn't care so much.
> (She lights another cigarette)

PEGGY
He's sweet.

CATRIONA

Too sweet. You can walk right over him.

PEGGY
(With a smile)
Do you?

CATRIONA

No. She does.

PEGGY

True. My Fred stands right up to Pa.

CATRIONA

For all the good it has done you. I wouldn't say
you're any closer to being married than I am.

PEGGY

Now, Catriona. . . .

CATRIONA

Do you mind plain speaking?

PEGGY
(Sits and shakes her head slowly)
Not really.

CATRIONA

Your father walks right over you, Mrs. Campbell
walks right over my George.

PEGGY

Don't say that.

CATRIONA
(She's up with a bound)
Why not? It's true. We're women. Sit and wait,

wait forever. Why should we?

PEGGY
We're supposed to.

CATRIONA
But what are we waiting for?
          (She starts to pace again)
For your father to agree to pay a stranger to do what
he can have you do for nothing. Waiting for Mrs.
Campbell herself to be willing to go live with her
sister in Glasgow so I can move into a house she
thinks is hers, and love her son? What's respect-
able in doing without? I'd rather do with. I'll find
my respect later for what I've won.

PEGGY
Catriona!

CATRIONA
Don't sound shocked. You know it's true. You'll
wait, too, you'll see.

PEGGY
Pa promised he'd say the word when the time is
right.

CATRIONA
The time will be right when he's . . .
          (She stops)

PEGGY
He's been good to me.

CATRIONA
I'm sorry for you. Unless you break out . . .
break out of all this . . . you'll never have Fred.

Never, ever, ever, no, he won't do it.

PEGGY
I can't believe Pa would do that to me.

CATRIONA
Persuade him.

PEGGY
We can't, we've tried, and he's so set in his ways.
          (The thought occurs)
Of course, oh, I couldn't do that?

CATRIONA
          (Eagerly, sensing the opening)
Do what? Go on, say it.

PEGGY
What would happen if I didn't do things just so?

CATRIONA
Ohhh?

PEGGY
If the tea were too strong, his toast too cold . . .

CATRIONA
Burn the gravy!

PEGGY
Hard potatoes . . . weak coffee . . .

CATRIONA
Soggy bacon . . .

PEGGY
Because I'm in love.

CATRIONA

Everyone knows a girl just can't think when she's in love.

PEGGY

You just come all unstuck.

CATRIONA

Go to pieces.

PEGGY

I just can't think . . . without Fred.

CATRIONA

Oh, Peggy . . .
          (Giving her a quick hug)
It might work.

PEGGY

If I can't have my Fred, well--we'll just have to see about that.

CATRIONA

Will you do it?

PEGGY

If I have to.

CATRIONA

I'll bet you won't. You'll wait, forever, but I won't. I've waited long enough. George won't ever get to it. I might just as well face up to it. After all-- he isn't the only man in the world.

PEGGY

Catriona!

CATRIONA

It's true. Why spend our lives as a door-scrape, where men kick the mud off their dirty boots? I love George dear; but for how long?

PEGGY

You love forever, just one.

CATRIONA

Oh, no, Peggy! You love till hope dies, then you love again. We're women. We have to love. I won't wait . . . waiting for Mrs. Campbell to open the front door, to smile at me. She'll never do that. If it's true about the whisky ship, then soon there'll be young men down to the hotel, some fun, a little happiness. Perhaps I'll go down to the hotel and see what I can do.

PEGGY

(Rising)
You aren't yourself.

CATRIONA

Maybe this is myself.
     (She picks up her coat and scarf)
There are other men besides George, and other girls, too. There's Jemima Ross. She's the one Mrs. Campbell approves of, plain and stupid, dressed in black. I've got her to fight. I know that, even if George doesn't. George, poor George, dear, sweet, kind and soft, so soft. I could love him dear if he were mine, but can he ever be mine? . . .

PEGGY

He can, he can.

CATRIONA

He can't. Perhaps if they've gotten a bottle or two,

then by now . . .

PEGGY
(As CATRIONA puts on her coat and scarf)
Catriona, you're . . .

CATRIONA
Speaking the truth. I like you, for all the sweet
dreams you have that won't ever be. But I will not
wait. I'm not that kind. I'm going down to the hotel.
I can cock an eyebrow, flick my hair and kick my
skirt with the best of them. If George wants me,
he can come to find me and speak his mind.

LOOK BACK IN ANGER

by

John Osborne

ALISON PORTER is the most elusive personal-
ity to catch in Mr. Osborne's brilliant play which
is so filled with anger, satire and invective. She
is tuned to a different key, a key of well-bred ma-
laise that is often drowned in the robust orchestra-
tion of her husband Jimmy and Cliff. She is in her
twenties and the combined physical oddity of the two
men makes her beauty more striking than it really
is. She manages to look quite elegant in her rather
grubby clothes. She is tall and slim. There is a
surprising reservation about her eyes which are so
large and deep they should make equivocation impossible. In our scene from Act Three she looks
rather ill and her hair is untidy.

HELENA CHARLES is the same age as Alison
and in the beginning of the play carefully and expen-
sively dressed. Now and again, when she allows her
rather judicial expression of alertness to soften,
she is very attractive. Her sense of matriarchal
authority makes most men who meet her anxious not
only to please but impress, as if she were the gracious representative of visiting royalty. In this
case, the royalty of that middle-class womanhood
which is so eminently secure in its divine rights
that it can afford to tolerate the parliament, and
reasonable free assembly, of its menfolk. Even
from other young women, like Alison, she receives
her due of respect and admiration. In our scene
she is dressed much like Alison. She looks more
attractive than before, for the setting of her face is
more relaxed. She still looks quite smart, but in
an unpremeditated, careless way.

The scene takes place in the Porters' attic apartment. HELENA is standing left of the table. ALISON is sitting on the arm-chair. From across the landing comes the sound of Jimmy's jazz trumpet. ALI-SON bends down to pick up a little pile of ash which has dropped from Jimmy's pipe. She drops it in the ashtray on the chair arm.

ALISON

He still smokes this foul old stuff. I used to hate it at first, but you get used to it.

HELENA

Yes.

ALISON

I went to the pictures last week, and some old man was smoking it in front, a few rows away. I actu-ally got up, and sat right behind him.

HELENA
(Coming down with cup of tea)
Here, have this.

ALISON
(Taking it)
Thanks.

HELENA

Are you sure you feel all right now?

ALISON
(Nods)
It was just--oh, everything. I must be mad, com-ing here like this. I'm sorry, Helena.

HELENA

Why should you be sorry--you, of all people?

ALISON

Because it was unfair and cruel of me to come back.
(Sips her tea)
So many times, I've just managed to stop myself
coming here--right at the last moment. Even today, when I went to the booking office, it was like
a charade, and I never believed that I'd let myself
walk onto that train. But once I got here, there
was nothing I could do. I had to convince myself
that everything I remembered about this place had
really happened to me once.
(She lowers her cup, and her foot plays
with the newspapers on the floor)
How many times in these past few months I've thought
of the evenings we used to spend here in this room.
Suspended and rather remote. You make a good
cup of tea.

HELENA
(Sitting left of the table)
Something Jimmy taught <u>me</u>.

ALISON
(Covering her face)
Oh, why am I here! You must all wish me a thou-
sand miles away!

HELENA

I don't wish anything of the kind. You've more
right to be here than I.

ALISON

Oh, Helena, don't bring out the book of rules----

HELENA

You are his wife, aren't you? Whatever I have done, I've never been able to forget that fact. You have all the rights----

ALISON

Helena--even I gave up believing in the divine rights of marriage long ago. They've got something different now--constitutional monarchy. You are where you are by consent. And if you start trying any strong-arm stuff, you're out. And I'm out.

HELENA

Is that something you learnt from him?

ALISON

Don't make me feel like a blackmailer, please! I've done something foolish, and rather vulgar in coming here tonight. But I did not come here in order to gain anything. You must believe that.

HELENA

Oh, I believe it, all right. That's why everything seems more wrong and terrible than ever. I feel so--ashamed.

ALISON

You talk as though he were something you'd swindled me out of----

HELENA
(Fiercely)

And you talk as if he were a book or something you pass around to anyone who happens to want it for five minutes. What's the matter with you? You sound as though you were quoting him all the time. I thought you told me once you couldn't bring yourself to believe in him.

ALISON

I don't think I ever believed in your way, either.

HELENA

At least, I still believe in right and wrong! Not
even the months in this madhouse have stopped me
doing that. Even though everything I have done is
wrong, at least I have known it was wrong.

ALISON

You loved him, didn't you? That's what you wrote,
and told me.

HELENA

And it was true.

ALISON

It was pretty difficult to believe at the time.

HELENA

I could hardly believe it myself. There doesn't
seem much point in trying to explain everything,
does there?

ALISON

Not really.

HELENA

Do you know--I have discovered what is wrong with
Jimmy? It's very simple really. He was born out
of his time.

ALISON

Yes, I know.

HELENA

There's no place for people like that any longer.
That's why he's so futile. Sometimes, when I listen to him, I feel he thinks he's still in the middle
of the French Revolution. And that's where he
ought to be, of course. He doesn't know where he
is, or where he's going.

ALISON

We seem to have had this conversation before.

HELENA

Yes, I remember everything you said about him.
It horrified me. I couldn't believe that you could
have married someone like that. Alison--it's all
over between Jimmy and me. I can see it now.
I've got to get out. No--listen to me. He wants
one world, and I want another, and lying in that bed
won't ever change it!

ALISON

Helena--you're not going to leave him?

HELENA

Yes. I am.
          (Before ALISON can interrupt, she goes
          on)
Oh, I'm not stepping aside to let you come back.
You can do what you like. Frankly, I think you'd
be a fool--but that's your own business. I think
I've given you enough advice.

ALISON

But he--he'll have no one.

HELENA

Oh, my dear, he'll find somebody. He'll probably

hold court here like one of the Renaissance popes.
Oh, I know I'm throwing the book of rules at you,
as you call it, but, believe me, you're never going
to be happy without it. I tried throwing it away all
these months, but I know now it just doesn't work.
When you came in at that door, ill and tired and
hurt, it was all over for me. You see--I didn't
know about the baby. It was such a shock. It's like
a judgment on us.

ALISON

You saw me, and I had to tell you what had happened. I lost the child. It's a simple fact. There
is no judgment, there's no blame----

HELENA

Maybe not. But I feel it just the same.

ALISON

But don't you see? It isn't logical.

HELENA

No, it isn't.
          (Calmly)
But I know it's right.
          (The trumpet gets louder)

ALISON

Helena--
          (Going to her)
--you mustn't leave him. He needs you----

HELENA

Do you think so?

ALISON

Maybe you're not the right one for him--we're

neither of us right----

HELENA
(Moving upstage)
Oh, why doesn't he stop that damned noise?

ALISON
(Sits in Helena's chair)
He wants something quite different from us. What
it is exactly I don't know--a kind of cross between
a mother and a Greek courtesan, a henchwoman, a
mixture of Cleopatra and Boswell. But give him a
little longer----

HELENA
Please! Will you stop that! I can't think!
          (There is a slight pause, and the trumpet
          goes on. She puts her hands to her head)
Jimmy, for God's sake!
          (It stops)
Jimmy, I want to speak to you........

ALISON
(Rising)
He doesn't want to see me.

HELENA
Stay where you are, and don't be silly. I'm sorry.
It won't be very pleasant, but I've made up my mind
to go, and I've got to tell him now.

NINE COACHES WAITING

by

Guy Bolton

from the novel by

Mary Stewart

LINDA MARTIN is a pretty and capable English girl in her twenties. She has been hired as governess for Philippe, a small boy, at the Chateau Valmy in France.

BERTHE is a maid at Valmy. She is a girl of local origin, a not-very-bright but pleasant creature. She is attractive and longs to win the heart of the man she loves--Bernard. "Nine Coaches Waiting" is a modern Gothic romance. The mounting danger to Philippe has reached a high point as this scene begins in the second act.

> LINDA is on stage and, after a moment, BERTHE appears and, in a little rush, comes stumbling into her arms. BERTHE is distraught and weeping hopelessly.

LINDA
Berthe! What is it? What's the matter?
> (BERTHE just shakes her head and rubs her sleeve across her eyes)

Take your time, Berthe.
> (She takes Berthe's hand in hers)

Why, you're freezing! Shall I make you some coffee?

BERTHE
(Making an effort to control her sobs)
No--nothing. I must tell you. I know I must.

LINDA
(Drawing her to a chair)
Sit down.
(She seats herself near BERTHE and leans
forward anxiously)
What happened?

BERTHE
It was Bernard. He was drinking and afterward
. . . he began talking.
(She licks her lips)
He was boasting kind of wild-like about when we
would be married. I'd be a princess, he said, and
we'd have money, a lot of money, and we'd buy a
farm and be rich.

LINDA
(Baffled)
Buy a farm----

BERTHE
Oh, ma'amzelle, he talked so wild and silly that I
got frightened and told him not to be a fool and
where would the likes of him get money to buy a
farm. And he said----
(Her voice falters and she wipes away
more tears)

LINDA
(Anxiously)
Go on. He said?

BERTHE
He said there'd be plenty of money later on . . .

when Philippe--when Philippe----

LINDA
(Half shaking her)
Yes?

BERTHE
When he's dead.

LINDA
Go on!

BERTHE
He said Monsieur de Valmy had promised him the money----

LINDA
Yes?

BERTHE
When Philippe is dead.

LINDA
Berthe!

BERTHE
Yes, ma'amzelle.

LINDA
(In tones icy with self-control)
You must finish now, Berthe. Philippe . . . so Philippe is going to die later on, is he? How much later on?

BERTHE
Bernard said soon. He said it's got to be soon because Monsieur Hubert cabled he's coming home

tomorrow. It's now or never, he said, and they
mustn't fail this time.

                    LINDA
This time?

                    BERTHE
They tried before, ma'amzelle. Like when Bernard
took Philippe to Chillon. He was to do it then--an
accident-like with the boat. They said he talked
too much and made you suspicious. That's why
they're not trusting him to do it this time. They
daren't risk another failure.

                    LINDA
Who are "they"?

                    BERTHE
The Valmys.   Monsieur and Madame and Mon-
sieur----

                    LINDA
        (Sharply)
No! No!

                    BERTHE
Yes, ma'amzelle. Monsieur Raoul, too.

                    LINDA
I don't believe it!
        (BERTHE shrugs)
Are you sure?
        (Another lift of the shoulders)
Wait here!
        (LINDA rises decisively)

                    BERTHE
        (Sharply)

Where are you going?
>   (Without pausing to reply, LINDA exits
>   swiftly to Philippe's room and a moment
>   later returns)
Is he all right?

LINDA
>   (Nods)
Asleep.   And now . . .   what next?

BERTHE
I don't know.

LINDA
Think!   Bernard told you so much he must have
dropped some hint!   You said Monsieur Hubert'll
get here tomorrow . . .
>   (Glances at her watch)
But that's today!   It's past midnight!   Do you realize that?
>   (Triumphantly)
And Monsieur Raoul's gone to Bellevigne.   That
proves he can't be in it!   And Monsieur de Valmy'll
probably keep well out of it since he's the person
who stands most obviously to gain.   So that leaves
Madame, since Raoul's not here.

BERTHE
Are you sure?

LINDA
That it's Madame?   Of course I'm not.   But----

BERTHE
That he's gone?

LINDA
>   (The spirit going out of her)

What do you mean?

BERTHE
(With a little shrug)
Valmy's a big place.

LINDA
(Sitting down)
You mean . . . he may still be here somewhere
. . . hiding?
(BERTHE nods)
But he went. People must have seen him go!

BERTHE
Yes, he left. But he could have come back. There's
a thing called an alibi.

LINDA
I think I ought to tell you something, Berthe. I
know Monsieur Raoul better than anyone else does.
I'm engaged to marry him.

BERTHE
Oh, I know that, already. Everybody does. That's
why they're not worried about your talking or going
to the police. If Philippe dies then, one day, you'll
be Madame la Comtesse de Valmy.

LINDA
What do you mean?
(Her voice changes and thins as she understands)
So now I have a motive, too, and I'm a handy one
to pin the blame on if things go wrong? Is that what
you mean?

BERTHE
Yes, ma'amzelle. I didn't want to say anything--

you were so happy--but we all understood the reason right away.

LINDA
I don't know what you're hinting at--the reason
for what?

BERTHE
Why else should he ask you to marry him?

LINDA
(The flood of bitter comprehension full
upon her)
Why else indeed?

THE DIRECTOR SPEAKS
on
CHARACTERIZATION

Characterization, if built logically and soundly, should begin within. As the human being moves through the life experience, it is the cumulative effect of the inner mental and emotional experiences which gradually carve "character" on face and body. As you study the people about you, a practice the serious actor should constantly pursue, you will see that the scowling, unhappy face of a passer-by is the result, not the cause, of a lifetime of suspicion and/or selfishness.

Naturally we tend to enjoy most the faces we see created by happiness. Clear, unafraid eyes and a bright smile are nearly always outward evidence of good and useful lives.

If you will remember this simple lesson from life as you work on stage characters, you will not make the common error of starting with exteriors. I have seen otherwise capable directors err in this fashion. They are the ones who think that handing a player a cane, asking for a squeaky voice and a stooped posture will, per se, result in an adequate portrayal of age. One of these directors once said, "Do you know that in performance, his character was only a surface exhibition?"

Of course it was, for the actor did not begin with the creation of the proper emotional and mental values. As you work with these people in our scenes I hope you will begin properly. Try first to understand the quality of the man or woman. This involves much more than the type of person. You must never be content to play a "kind" of person--

for this descends quickly into the great pitfall of the stock company--casting a handful of actors into a series of "leads" or "juveniles," merely because they are on a payroll, forgetting completely any fidelity to truth in casting.

So you begin by establishing the variations in a character which make it different from anyone else, written or real. The playwright sets certain of these differences by the way he thinks and the way he writes. Then we have to consider the time of the play, the locale, the racial and national group to which the character belongs--and the position within that group. Then, a long list of factors which include: educational and social background, home life, life experience until the time of the play, any events which may have had strong effect upon the individual.

As you proceed in this work you will gradually gain a sense of how the character thinks--and how the character feels. Now you can begin to apply the emotional and thought patterns to the lines you have learned. Gradually, very gradually, a characterization should begin to evolve. If you do your work well, it may be moving toward uniqueness-- a person different from all others--as real life people are each wonderfully unique.

As you attain a growing command over the inner structure, you should begin to dress the exterior. Now you are ready for the additions of walk, posture, properties and make-up. Not only will they fit easily into the growing portrait at this point, but you ought to be far more expert in your selection than you could possibly have been when you first met the character and had to start learning words and meanings.

As the scene moves toward completion, you may ask the ancient question, "How much emotion should I feel?"

This has been a continuing debate in theatre for at least a century. In 1870, Diderot said that the good actor had to remain insensible to the emotion he was portraying. The opposite view was loudly stated by Constant Coquelin who held that the player "feels" the emotions during rehearsals but not in performance.

Then came Stanislavsky who said emotion should be felt in some degree through both rehearsals and performance!

I have always maintained, despite Monsieur Diderot, that acting without emotional content takes away what I consider the basic reason for living theatre, a communion of emotional experience by actors and audiences.

As I wrote in my book, Directing the Play from Selection to Opening Night, "We hold that theatre is a higher form of creative endeavor than the perfectly timed manipulations of the juggler, the ventriloquist, or the puppeteer; but the actor who uses only the exterior of a character can lay claim to being little more than these."

So I want you to feel the emotion you create and, with practice, the creative process should become more rapid--and more exact. If you go back once more to the "how much" in your question, I will ask you to accept this answer.

It will vary as widely as one human being varies from another in his imagination, emotional structure, mentality and life experience. So long as we deal with living players there can be no rigid level of emotion. Physical tests long ago proved that a dozen men of the same age, background and education, subjected to a simple example of pain, show a dozen levels of reaction on the graph.

And within yourself you will find the created emotion of a characterization varying slightly from performance to performance. How rare is the actor who has not at some time said, "This time I didn't feel it," and "Tonight I was really in the part."

This variation is true of all artistic creativity, from the painter who works over the bad brush-stroke to the writer who rips the page from the typewriter and crumples it away.

There are over-all emotional limits which range from the person who cannot create emotional values and, therefore, should not be allowed on any stage, to those who lack control and let emotions assume the command of full reality. When real anger or real fear appears, acting goes out the window.

To feel, yet not feel too much, this is your objective. Does it sound difficult? I am glad that it does, for acting is a complex process asking that we work in it with humility and perseverance. How else could we consider it as a worthy part of the art form which is living theatre?

TOM JONES

by

David Rogers

Based upon the Novel by
Henry Fielding

As Partridge, the "sometimes narrator," says, "Many people said TOM JONES was born to hang and others called hanging too good for him. But I say, Tom was a paragon of virtue--misunderstood as the good so often are in this wicked world. Our story takes place more than two hundred years ago when the world was, indeed, wicked, bawdy, and licentious. In short, a time like any other." TOM JONES is the dashing young man at the center of this highly entertaining story. The lovely SOPHIA is a pretty young lady who follows and finds TOM after he is banished from his home. LADY BELL-ASTON is older, a true lady of fashion of the period. The scene occurs in Lady Bellaston's drawing room. TOM is on stage when SOPHIA enters from left and sees him.

SOPHIA

Oh! What are you doing here?

TOM
(Rising, astounded)

Sophia!

SOPHIA
(Suspicious)

I did not know you were acquainted with Lady Bell-aston.

TOM
(Lying blatantly)
I only knew her name--
(Picks up the muff and crosses to her)
--which I read in your muff.
(Gives it to her)

SOPHIA
(Nonchalantly)
Oh, you found it.
(Lying in her turn)
I wondered where I dropped it.
(Changing the subject)
But by your clothing, Mr. Jones, you seem to have
turned into a gentleman of fashion. I wonder how
you managed that so quickly.

TOM
(Changing this subject)
Let us not, I beseech you, waste one of these precious moments in discussing clothing after this long
and terrible pursuit.

SOPHIA
(Cool)
Pursuit? Of whom?

TOM
Need I say, of you? Allow me, on my knees--
(Kneels)
--to beg your pardon.

SOPHIA
(Sarcastically)
My pardon? Why should you ask my pardon? Just
because I heard my name bandied about in a vulgar
tavern . . . and you supping with strange women.

TOM

Oh, my only love--
> (Rises)

--do me the justice to think I was never unfaithful to you. Though I despaired of ever seeing you again, I loved you.

SOPHIA

And that woman?

TOM

A mere companion for dinner to whom I spoke of nothing but my love for my Sophia.

SOPHIA

> (Melting)

Oh, Tom . . .
> (Allows him to embrace her)

TOM

And my hopes . . . to marry her.

SOPHIA

Marry you! Oh, Tom, I dare not even be seen with you. No one . . . not even Lady Bellaston . . . can be trusted not to tell my father, and should he hear, it would bring ruin on us both.

TOM

Ruin! No, I cannot act so base a part. Dearest Sophia, whatever it costs me, I shall renounce you.
> (Kisses her)

I will give you up.
> (Kisses her again)

My love I shall ever retain but from the distance of some foreign land where my voice, my sighs, my despairs, shall never reach your ears.

(Kisses her again)

(LADY BELLASTON enters D L)

LADY BELLASTON
(Sarcastically)
I thought, Miss Western, you had been at the play.
    (TOM and SOPHIA jump apart)

SOPHIA
I . . . I . . . left early. I thought it vulgar. It
was called Hamlet.

LADY BELLASTON
I should not have broken in upon you, Miss Western,
had I known you had . . . company.

SOPHIA
No, madam, our business was at an end. Surely
you remember, I have often mentioned the loss of
my muff, which--
    (Not wanting to say who he is)
--this strange gentleman having found was so kind
as to return to me.

LADY BELLASTON
(Sarcastically)
What good fortune. But how could you know, strange
gentleman, it was Miss Western's or where to find
her in London?

TOM
Her name and your address were written in it.

LADY BELLASTON
(To SOPHIA)
How clever of you to insure that all your . . .

possessions . . . can return to you.

TOM
It was the luckiest chance imaginable.

SOPHIA
Thank you so much, sir. The muff has great sentimental value to me.

TOM
I believe, madam, it is customary to give some reward on these occasions. I request no more than the honor of being permitted to pay another visit here.

LADY BELLASTON
I make no doubt you are a gentleman . . . by your clothes . . . which are strangely familiar . . . and my doors are never shut to people of fashion.

TOM
Your servant, ladies.
    (Bows and goes out D L)

LADY BELLASTON
Upon my word, a pretty young fellow. I wonder who he is.

SOPHIA
I wonder.

LADY BELLASTON
    (Laughing)
I vow you must forgive me, Sophia, but when I first came into the room, I suspected it was Mr. Jones himself.

SOPHIA
(Trying to pass it off, laughing)
Did your ladyship, indeed?

LADY BELLASTON
I can't think what put it into my head as he was gen-
teelly dressed, which I think is not commonly the
case with your friend.

SOPHIA
(Beginning to be upset)
I beg your ladyship not to tease me about Mr. Jones.

LADY BELLASTON
Why, Sophy, I shall begin to fear you are still in
love with the man.

SOPHIA
Upon my honor, I am as indifferent to Mr. Jones
as to that strange gentleman who just left us.

LADY BELLASTON
Upon my honor, I believe that.

SOPHIA
(Upset, afraid of being revealed)
Your ladyship's pardon, but I would retire to my
chamber.

LADY BELLASTON
No doubt you are weary after your evening at the
play.
            (SOPHIA goes out U R. LADY BELLAS-
            TON crosses to the table R and rings bell.
            To herself:)
That girl must be got out of the way.
            (Goes to the table L, takes up the pen and
            begins to write)

SEVEN DAYS IN MAY

by

Kristin Sergel

Based on the book by

Fletcher Knebel and Charles W. Bailey II

This suspense classic tells of a military conspiracy to take over the United States. A loyal few begin to suspect and then to analyze the frightening facts and their connotations. This scene in Act Two is in the office of the President of the United States at a moment when the plot seems almost unstoppable.

PRESIDENT JORDAN LYMAN is not only a man of high intelligence but one who also inspires confidence. He wears glasses.

SENATOR RAYMOND CLARK is the senator from Georgia. He is a good-humored man and a close friend of the President's.

CHRISTOPHER TODD is a hard-headed lawyer and deeply loyal to his country.

> The PRESIDENT is seated at his desk while TODD is in a chair at left. CLARK is pacing at right center.

CLARK
(He is finishing his account)
And that's about the size of it.
(He mops his face with a handkerchief)
I was planning to take a vacation in the desert but nossir, give me a swamp any time.

TODD

Ray, you said this Colonel Broderick offered to let you telephone Senator Prentice.

CLARK

I declined, for obvious reasons.

TODD

Mr. President, I think you should call Prentice at once--let's find out what he has to say about their putting a colleague under arrest.

LYMAN

Won't that tip our hand?

TODD

They already know we're on to it. A call from you might upset Prentice enough so you could get some information from him.
            (LYMAN frowns, buzzes his secretary)

LYMAN

Esther, get me Senator Prentice. . . .
            (After a pause, he speaks firmly into tele-
            phone)
Good morning, Fred, this is the President. I'd like to know about this private telephone line you have to a military base in New Mexico.
            (Tight-mouthed)
It's known as ECOMCON. . . . I see. . . . Of course. . . .
            (Holding back anger)
You've been as helpful as ever, Senator, and frankly I don't believe you.
            (He hangs up. To the others)
He's never heard of ECOMCON.

CLARK

Liar.

TODD

We can't even prove it exists.

CLARK

But we can. Jiggs' friend--Colonel Henderson.

LYMAN

What about him?

CLARK

After I talked him into letting me out of there, he
said he couldn't go back--he'd be finished. I took
him to my house.

TODD

We'd better have him here with us, Ray--he'll be
able to tell us how ECOMCON works.

CLARK

I'll phone my housekeeper.

LYMAN
(Buzzing Esther)
Esther, get Senator Clark's house on the phone. . . .

CLARK
(Taking the telephone)
Hate to do this--Henderson took quite a chance, fly-
ing the coop. Least I should do is let him sleep
late. . . .
(Into telephone)
Hello, Maggie? We have an overnight guest. . . .
Yes, I want you to rouse him as tactfully as possi-
ble, ask him to come to the phone. . . .

(Grim, unbelieving)

What? . . . Of course he was--I brought him in myself. . . . All right, Maggie. Forget it.

(He hangs up)

He's gone.

LYMAN

GONE?

CLARK

Without a trace. Henderson's been shanghaied! They're starting to play rough.

TODD

What's happened?

CLARK

ECOMCON exists all right--I found it. The minute I drove up, they put me under arrest. I managed to talk your friend into getting me out of the place and we hightailed it back to Washington. I took him to my house last night. Now he's left without a trace.

(Shakes his head emphatically)

He was scared stiff--he wouldn't have just walked away.

TODD

We've got to find him.

CLARK

They probably followed us from the airport. I kept telling him we don't use thugs in Washington. . . .

(Ruefully)

A lot I know. . . .

LYMAN

How far would they go?

CLARK
(Thinking a moment)
They could put him in a military guardhouse somewhere.   All they'd have to do is charge him with
going AWOL, something like that . . .

LYMAN
We've got to find him.

TODD
Mr. President, we'd better make a few decisions
right now.

LYMAN
What are you suggesting, Todd?

TODD
How you can break General Scott and preserve your
authority.   I've got a few ideas.

LYMAN
Let's hear them.

TODD
(Speaking quickly; he's thought this out
carefully)
First, I'd get General Garlock down here from
Mount Thunder--order him to put a 24-hour guard
on the radio and television controls--lock the gates
at Mount Thunder and let no one inside, military
or civilian--on pain of court martial.
(He pauses for breath)
Second, I'd call General Scott over here and fire
him----

LYMAN
(Interrupting)

And what's the excuse?

                        TODD
Unauthorized establishment of ECOMCON.

                        LYMAN
He could deny any knowledge of it.

                        TODD
                    (Ignoring this)
Third, I'd dismiss Hardesty, Dieffenbach and Riley
as members of the Joint Chiefs--for conspiring to
annul a treaty executed by the President and rati-
fied by the Senate.   Fourth, I'd install somebody I
trusted as Chairman of the Joint Chiefs, tell him
to cancel any orders for flying troops out of El Paso.
If planes had already gone out, I'd tell him to call
them back.

                        LYMAN
                (As TODD subsides momentarily)
That's quite a package, Todd.   Sure you didn't forget anything?

                        TODD
I'd also get a company from the Third Infantry and
station them around the White House.

                        LYMAN
And where is General Scott during all this?

                        TODD
Locked in a room in this house--under Secret Service guard.

                        LYMAN
                (After a pause, to CLARK)

What do you think, Ray?

CLARK
Well, it's a cinch the General couldn't run a revolution cooped up in a White House bedroom.

LYMAN
And how would I explain it to the rest of the country?

CLARK
He's in quarantine.   Smallpox.

TODD
We can't waste time joking, Ray.

LYMAN
He isn't joking.   Todd--the only thing wrong with your program is the same thing that was wrong with it last Tuesday.   The newspapers would go wild, yelling for my scalp.   Congress would come back in a rage.   Ten bills of impeachment would be introduced the first day.   They'd demand a court martial of General Scott--to "get the facts."
(He winces)
Before it was over they'd have me in St. Elizabeth's with half the head-shrinkers in the country certifying I was suffering with delusions of persecution.

TODD
(Heatedly, rising as he speaks)
Even granting all that--which I don't--the fact is, you took an oath to defend the Constitution of the United States.   Unless you act fast you'll be violating that oath.

LYMAN
(Barking)

Don't tell me about my oath. You may be a great
lawyer, but how I do my job is my business.

TODD
(Angrily)
This happens to be my country as well as yours,
Jordan--and I don't intend to stand by while it slips
away because you can't face reality.

LYMAN
(A tired voice)
You don't understand, Todd. No man who hasn't
gone to the voters could understand what's involved.

TODD
I've never noticed that the mere process of election
conferred wisdom on a man.

LYMAN
(Totally flat)
Todd, you couldn't be elected dogcatcher.

TODD
(Bitingly)
At least we know where we stand, Mr. President.
(They glare at each other, and CLARK in-
tervenes)

CLARK
(To TODD)
Take it easy, boy. He's trying to tell you what
would happen if we blast this thing out into the open.
It'll tear the country apart . . . believe me.

TODD
All right, we can't come out in the open.
(He takes something out of his brief case

and waves it at LYMAN)
This tax return Casey put us onto is enough to force
General Scott's resignation, and I don't care if it
is blackmail!

LYMAN
I've told you I can't use it!
(The desk buzzer sounds)

TODD
(As LYMAN answers)
But it's all we've got!

LYMAN
(Answering)
Yes? . . . General Rutkowski's HERE? . . . Send
him in.
(Clicks off)

TODD
For Heaven's sake, Jordan--Scott's committed
treason, not to mention kidnaping. . . .

LYMAN
We can't fight fire with mud, Todd--and that's final.
Rutkowski's coming in. He's head of our Air De-
fense Command, and he's NOT part of the betting
pool.

STARDUST

by

Walter Kerr

This gay comedy tells of a hard-working and attractive actress who comes to play the lead in a summer production at a small university somewhere in New Hampshire. The students who play her supporting roles are much too ardent disciples of Stanislavsky. The conflict between the actress and the students leads to amusing moments, as we see in this scene from Act Three.

CLAIRE is the best friend of the actress, PRUDENCE. She is in her middle thirties, smartly dressed, and retaining much of the attractiveness that was hers when she was a mainstay in a good stock company, mostly doing comedy. She has common sense, a deadly sense of humor, and a workable imagination.

ARTHUR SCOTT, Jr. is a handsome young man--in a slightly stuffy sort of way. He dresses flawlessly, and is smug.

JERRY FLANAGAN is thirty, sandy-haired, and nice-looking. He is wise in the ways of the theatre, and has always been. He is completely unexcitable, always casual, and never unpleasant, even when being sarcastic.

PRUDENCE MASON, the actress, is nice, wholesome, and perfectly sensible, contrary to all expectation. She is in her late twenties.

The play occurs in the combination office and studio of the Drama Department--which, at this college, is called "The Academy of Dramatic and Allied Arts."

It is about nine-twenty on the night of the performance. CLAIRE is busy folding one of Prudence's
costumes. She takes it into the office down right
which is now serving as Prudence's dressing-room.
She returns to a desk at right center which is now
Prudence's make-up table. She is humming and
occasionally glances apprehensively in the direction
of the school's stage which is off upper left. After
a moment ARTHUR enters from left.

CLAIRE

Well, if it isn't Junior! How's business?

ARTHUR
(With sullen dignity)

I'm going to wait here till the first act's over. It
is almost.
(He speaks scornfully)
Unless you have some objection.

CLAIRE

Not at all. But I warn you. If you so much as lay
a finger on me, you'll answer to Captain Mulroy,
of the Mounted.

ARTHUR
(Sitting, disconsolately)

I don't know why people think you're funny.

CLAIRE
(Letting it pass)

Prudence get a big hand on her entrance?
(ARTHUR nods, morosely)
How's she doing?

ARTHUR

I didn't wait to see. I couldn't sit there and watch

her, when she hasn't let me see her for three whole days. Have you had anything to do with that?

CLAIRE
(With astonished innocence)
Me? Why, I haven't done anything except stop the telephone service and lock the door!

ARTHUR
Why should she take it out on me? I'm the one who ought to be indignant!

CLAIRE
Go ahead. Be indignant. Stamp your sore foot.

ARTHUR
Nobody's explained to my satisfaction the things that went on here the other night!

CLAIRE
Well, it was like this. There we were--trapped in this salt mine. No water anywhere. The rescue squad forty miles away. Suddenly I felt my mind going--going----

ARTHUR
Oh, cut it out!
(He whirls on her, furious)
I've got to have a showdown!........
(There is a burst of applause in the distance)

CLAIRE
There's the curtain. It's over, the first act!

(She goes out up left center as JERRY rushes in from left)

JERRY
She come off yet?

ARTHUR

No. Claire's gone after her. What is all this?

JERRY

Those crazy kids! The juvenile, jackass stupidity!

ARTHUR

What are they doing to Prudence?

JERRY

They're stealing the show, en masse!

ARTHUR

How?

JERRY

As far as I can figure it out, it's a combination of upstaging, downstaging, and the lateral pass.

ARTHUR

I don't understand those words.

JERRY

About ten minutes ago, somebody slipped her a bad cue. It threw her, but she came out of it all right. Then as soon as she got started again, they cut into her speeches and tramped all over her lines. Then they started rewriting the show, leaving her out!

ARTHUR

That's awful!

JERRY

Then they started marching. When she'd come downstage to force a line through to the audience, they'd move upstage in a body, making her turn her back. And when she went upstage, to counter, they

marched down and got in front of her, blotting her
out completely. It's worse than an All-Star Bene-
fit! And that's not all! . . .

(CLAIRE rushes in, up center from left, and
dashes toward the desk down right)

CLAIRE

Flanagan! Get me some ice water.
　　(JERRY starts for the door left)
And a machine gun!
　　(JERRY runs out, left. CLAIRE rummages
　　through Prudence's things feverishly, snatch-
　　ing up a towel)

ARTHUR

I hope you're satisfied. If she'd come away with
me, this wouldn't have happened!

CLAIRE

(Throwing the towel at him)
Shut up, and hold this! Where's that ammonia?

(As ARTHUR catches the towel and CLAIRE
keeps searching in a frenzy, PRUDENCE appears from up left. She is humiliated, and
nearly white with anger, trembling all over.
She is in costume for Cleopatra, but her make-
up has begun to run. She looks awful)

PRUDENCE

They hate me. They hate me!

CLAIRE

(Starting to her with the ammonia bottle)
Here, baby, sniff some of this.

PRUDENCE
(Staring straight front, paying no attention)
All right. All right! I hate them, too! I'll fix
them. I'll get even! I'll see that none of them ever
gets near Broadway! I'll go to every manager in
New York. I'll tell Equity. I'll keep them out of
Hollywood. I'll--I'll write a letter to the Sunday
Times!
   (She starts to cry)

CLAIRE
Sure, baby. We'll chop them up and scatter the
pieces from an aeroplane.

PRUDENCE
What they did to me! What--they--did--to--me!

ARTHUR
(Smugly)
That's your theatre for you, Prudence.

PRUDENCE
And the lights! Every time I got in one, it went
off.

ARTHUR
It's outrageous! I wouldn't put up with it!

CLAIRE
(Quickly, before he plants this idea)
Come on, honey. You've only got fifteen minutes
for the change.

ARTHUR
You don't expect her to go back out there--with
those neurotics!

CLAIRE
You think she can't hold her own? Give her five minutes and a fresh start, and she'll play them right off the stage!

PRUDENCE
(The horror still with her)
You don't know what it's like!

CLAIRE
All right. I'll hop into a costume myself and go on with you, in every scene. One false move and they'll never know what hit them.

PRUDENCE
(Pulling away from CLAIRE)
Don't be ridiculous!

ARTHUR
The time has come to put a stop to this whole business!

PRUDENCE
(Running to him)
Arthur! You're the only one I can lean on!

ARTHUR
(His arm around her, her head buried)
I certainly am!

CLAIRE
If his suit runs, it'll be tough on your make-up.

PRUDENCE
And I've been so mean to you! What would I do without you now?

ARTHUR
Darned if I know!

CLAIRE
She'd get into her next costume, go back out there, and make those kids look sick!

ARTHUR
What for? Nobody has to put up with this!

PRUDENCE
(Her mouth becoming set)
No, they certainly don't.

ARTHUR
All those kids have done since she came here is make her unhappy and hysterical, and do dumb things like the other night. Even dragging me into it. And now this!
(He speaks firmly)
You're coming away with me!

PRUDENCE
(Dazed, not knowing her own mind)
Am I?

CLAIRE
(Going to PRUDENCE, taking her hand)
No, she's got to go back out there.

ARTHUR
Why? She doesn't owe those kids anything!

CLAIRE
Not them, Wall Street. The audience. You don't walk out on a show in the middle of a performance.

ARTHUR

This isn't a performance.　It's a catastrophe!

PRUDENCE
(Her jaw set)

You're right, Arthur.　I couldn't face it.　I'm going with you.

CLAIRE

Honey, listen!

PRUDENCE
(Whirling on her)

And don't you tell me the show must go on! There's no law of the theatre that says it must go on with me under it!

(JERRY runs in from left with a pitcher of ice water)

JERRY

Here's the ice water!　I got it at a lecture in the Commerce Building.　I had to swipe it off the speaker's stand, but I got it!

CLAIRE

Save it for the Professor.　When he hears this, he'll need it.

JERRY

Hears what?

PRUDENCE

I'm leaving.
(She starts for the office down right)

Claire, help me out of this dress.

JERRY

Miss Mason! What about "Christina"?

PRUDENCE

(Harassed)

I'm--I'm going back with Arthur.

JERRY

But you can still have that contract!

ARTHUR

Prudence doesn't want Hollywood charity.

JERRY

There's no such thing. What about it, Miss Mason?

PRUDENCE

I'm sorry, Mr. Flanagan. I'm so mixed up. I'll
--just have to quit, that's all.

THE BRASS BUTTERFLY

by

William Golding

The scene is the Emperor's villa on the Isle of Capri. It is a late summer afternoon some time in the third century A.D. Everything is in good taste but the setting is unspecific.

In this scene from Act Two we meet five of the interesting characters. The SERGEANT is a professional soldier.

The EMPEROR is, of course, Caesar, and the play occurs at his summer home.

POSTUMUS is Caesar's bloodthirsty, Christian-killing heir apparent.

MAMILLIUS is Caesar's gentle grandson, who is changing from boy to man.

The Egyptian, PHANOCLES, is an inventor whose creations include a steamboat, a cannon and a pressure cooker.

As in "Lord of the Flies," playwright Golding pits intelligence against irrationality, civilization against savagery, and gives us a comedy as thought-provoking as it is laugh-provoking.

The EMPEROR, POSTUMUS, MAMILLIUS and PHANOCLES are on stage when the Sergeant's voice is heard.

SERGEANT
(Off R)
General . . . General Posthumus----

POSTUMUS
What was that? Who's there?

SERGEANT
(Off R)
Sir! Sir!

POSTUMUS
(Draws sword)
Stay where you are, everybody! I'm here, man!

(Enter bleeding SERGEANT)

SERGEANT
The men, sir! Something horrible, sir!

POSTUMUS
Who sent you? Who is your officer?

SERGEANT
The officer's dead, sir. Drowned.

POSTUMUS
Make your report, Sergeant.

SERGEANT
We were in the other ship, sir--not yours----

EMPEROR
The other ship?

SERGEANT
Yes, Caesar. Our two were in advance of the fleet.
We got orders to burn the magic ship, so we got
alongside----

POSTUMUS
Sergeant! Make your report to me!

SERGEANT
Yes, sir. The boarding was dead easy, sir. The

Captain shouts, "Oars!" and out went the oars, straight and firm and level as a road. Then comes a shout--"Boarders, away!" and we all charges out along the oars and on to the magic ship. There was hardly any crew to speak of for a ship of that size, and what there was we knocks on the head with no trouble at all . . .

POSTUMUS

Come to the point quickly. What happened to my men?

SERGEANT

Well, sir, we set her on fire, sir, like you said-- and she burnt like a volcano!

POSTUMUS

Then you sank her?

SERGEANT

Yes, sir--but not before she woke up and went mad.

POSTUMUS

Went mad?

SERGEANT

She was alive, sir--I swear it! The few that es- caped and are able to talk will bear me out. When the flames got hold, sir, they made her big brass belly scream at us, and those wooden wheels went 'round. She moved, sir--I swear she did--of her own accord--moved through the water without row- ers or the wind! Then those wheels caught us, sir, and we were set on fire, and then she swung 'round faster and faster and chewed up your ship, just as if she was a giant shark, sir! The sea was full of men drowning and burning and screaming, and the ship was screaming, and I was screaming--we were all screaming----

POSTUMUS

Company Sergeant Pyrrhus, Leading Sergeant of "A" Company in the invincible Roman Army of General Postumus--'shun!
     (The SERGEANT comes to attention)
That's better! Now stand at ease and tell me how many escaped.

SERGEANT

Not much more than a dozen, sir--not fighting fit, that is . . . they were burnt a bit, most of 'em--I'm senior, sir.

POSTUMUS

I see. I'm glad you're safe, Sergeant.
     (Crossing to PHANOCLES)
So you were altering the circumstance of life, were you? And you altered it at the cost of nearly two hundred of my men. I shall let their comrades try you. They will know best how to alter what is left of your life!
     (To EMPEROR)
And you, Caesar, plotted nothing with this Greek monstrosity--or with this little fancy bastard! Oh, no! You just wanted to see how fierce your little pet could look in such pretty armor--and with purple frills, too!

EMPEROR

Postumus, a thought has just come to me. You have been--how shall I put it----

MAMILLIUS

--bluffing.

EMPEROR

Yes, I wondered why I'd heard no drums. You are separated from your fleet. You arrived with only two ships and now they are both sunk.

MAMILLIUS

You've been hurrying on, Postumus--getting there first--moving with terrified speed----

POSTUMUS

What if I have? The fleet will be here in a few hours, and I've men enough to hold the quay and you haven't even a guard! Ships that go mad--armor--explosives--whatever they might be! Sergeant!

SERGEANT

Sir?

POSTUMUS

Could you aim that catapult?

SERGEANT

I did fifteen years with the Mark Seven, sir.

POSTUMUS

Train it around away from the sea. Aim it inland, aim it at this villa, for that matter--a big hole you said, Phanocles? Flames and smoke?

PHANOCLES

This is a nightmare . . .

SERGEANT

Do I loose it, sir?

POSTUMUS

No--let's just train it around, Sergeant. If we have

to fire it, we shall wait till the fleet arrives. We must let all the troops share in the fun.

SERGEANT

Yes, sir.

POSTUMUS

Meanwhile, stand guard within earshot and keep your sword drawn.

SERGEANT

Sir!

(Exit)

POSTUMUS

You know me, Caesar.

EMPEROR

Indeed, I thought I did.

MAMILLIUS

I know him, Grandfather. He's frightened.

POSTUMUS

I? Frightened? There is reason for you to be frightened, Mamillius. I'm arresting you!

MAMILLIUS

Try!

POSTUMUS

Do you think you can fight me?

EMPEROR

Postumus--Phanocles is right. This is a nightmare. Neither I nor the boy wish you any harm. You are Heir Designate. What more do you want?

POSTUMUS

You had both better prepare to sail with me to
Rome. As for the boy--he is under arrest. Give
me your sword.

>   (MAMILLIUS draws his sword)

MAMILLIUS

Come and take it!

POSTUMUS

Is it possible he wants me to run him through?

EMPEROR

Postumus, this is open rebellion!

POSTUMUS

>   (Laughs)

Caesar, if you're sensible, the whole thing can be
disposed of with a minimum of fuss.

EMPEROR

What do you propose?

POSTUMUS

Consent to the arrest of this boy.

EMPEROR

And then?

POSTUMUS

Then you may remain in your villa and I shall go to
Rome with your signed appointment of me as Regent
--or co-ruler, if you prefer the old forms.

EMPEROR

And then?

POSTUMUS

What then?

EMPEROR

The boy?

POSTUMUS

Surely you must realize, Caesar----

EMPEROR

--that he would die quickly--or perhaps slowly----

POSTUMUS

Before that, he would have a fair, unbiased trial.

EMPEROR

What do you think of my health?

POSTUMUS

Good for your age.

EMPEROR

What would you think of it after I signed such a
document?

POSTUMUS

Frankly, I should cease to think of it.

EMPEROR

It would probably be given into the care of others.
I should have perhaps a month to live!

POSTUMUS

I'm a ruler, and I'm a Roman. You, Greek--come
down to the quay with me.

MAMILLIUS

No, Phanocles--get behind me!

POSTUMUS

Why, Mamillius! Both I and my agent underestimated you. So much the worse for you!

MAMILLIUS

I intend to live as long as I can.

POSTUMUS

Mamillius, come and look out there--come on! What do you see?

MAMILLIUS

Water!

POSTUMUS

Look at the horizon.

MAMILLIUS

Ships.

POSTUMUS

My ships, Mamillius. Nine thousand men.

MAMILLIUS

Coward!

POSTUMUS

For making sure? Enjoy yourself, Mamillius. When the men land I shall sweep this island in force and form. You have rather less than three hours to live.

EMPEROR

Wait! Postumus, I beg you, let us come to some composition.

POSTUMUS

Before he drew his little sword I might have. But

why should I argue now? My ships do that for me.
        (Exit POSTUMUS)

MAMILLIUS
What shall we do?

EMPEROR
Phanocles could not arrange for our sudden trans-
portation through the air to Rome?

PHANOCLES
No, Caesar.

EMPEROR
Then we must eat, drink, and be quietly merry.

MAMILLIUS
Eat? I could not eat.

EMPEROR
But I think with such clarity when eating. Something may yet be done. Besides, Phanocles, we
were to dine together tonight to try your new pressure cooker. Very well, then--the canceled dinner
is redecreed. We shall try the pressure cooker!

VOICE
        (Off L as the fanfare starts)
The canceled demonstra----

Index

Preface: Before the Curtain.....................9

The Director Speaks on

Memorization..............................35
Variety in Line Reading.....................51
Listening.................................82
Concentration.............................112
Characterization..........................137

Plays

Agamemnon...............................41
The Brass Butterfly.......................166
Cyrano de Bergerac.......................20
The Entertainer...........................31
Epitaph for George Dillon..............44, 91
The Great Big Doorstep....................101
Hamlet...................................27
Look Back in Anger...................17, 122
Luther...............................22, 84
A Man Called Peter........................62
The Menaechmi............................48
The Mouse That Roared.....................55
Nine Coaches Waiting......................130
Portrait of Jennie........................75
Rally Round the Flag, Boys!................68
Seven Days in May.........................147
The Song of Bernadette....................37
A Sound of Hunting........................106
Stardust.................................156
Tight Little Island.......................114
Tom Jones................................141